Spouses

of the World

Bullet Dodging Behind Diplomatic Glamour

Edited by
Linn Eleanor Zhang

SABRESTORM
STORIES

Edited, designed and typeset by Sabrestorm Stories Ltd.

British Library Cataloguing in Publication Data
A catalogue record for this book is available from the
British Library

Published by Sabrestorm Stories Ltd., The Olive Branch,
Caen Hill, Devizes, Wiltshire SN10 1RB United Kingdom.
Company number 11927154.

Website: www.sabrestormstories.com
Email: enquiries@sabrestormstories.co.uk

ISBN 978-1-913163-01-3

Spouses of the World

of the World

Bullet Dodging Behind Diplomatic Glamour

Edited by
Linn Eleanor Zhang

Written by
Agnes Fenyvesy
Amy Richardson
Britten Holter
Carmen Davies
Emilia Atmanagara
Ilona Kenkadze
Julia Gajewska-Pratt
M Mohammed
Marzia Brofferio Celeste
Monica Pavese Rubins
Nina Rousu
Olga Lucia Lozano
Ratna Roshida Ab Razak
Valentina Prevolnik Rupel & Manca Rupel
Zoofa Talha

Table of Contents

Acknowledgements

We thank the British Academy/Leverhulme Small Research Grants and Loughborough University for funding and supporting this book project.

The pursuit of this book would not have been possible without the support of our families. We would like to thank all the diplomats, diplomatic children and parents standing behind the spouses in this book. And we send special thanks to Anu Holter, Cindy Renggli, Gwen Bairstow, Ramune Muraliene and members of the Book Club of the Finnish Spousal Association, who have provided the team with valuable feedback on earlier drafts.

We thank Dr Birgit Pauksztat for her unfaltering faith in our work during the long journey of producing this book, which would not have been created without her.

We also thank the Diplomatic Spouse Club London and the Diplomatic Service Families Association, Foreign, Commonwealth & Development Office, UK.

Thanks must also go to Margarita Mavromichalis, a diplomatic spouse and award-winning photographer whose photographs used in this book have captured some of the emotions of being a diplomatic spouse.

The editor would also like to thank Prof Anne-Wil Harzing and Prof Jeff Hearn for encouraging and supporting her to pursue this book throughout the years.

Forewords

Marina Wheeler

In 2017-18, I had the privilege to meet a number of the contributors to this book. Their spouses had been posted to London and I, at the time, was married to Boris Johnson, then the UK's Foreign Secretary.

We shared convivial times, at formal receptions and also events organised by the newly founded and energetically-run, Diplomatic Spouses Club of London.

I was struck then, as I am again when reading these accounts, by the enthusiasm and accomplishments of these diplomatic wives (as they still mostly are).

Life on the diplomatic circuit can be glamorous and exciting, much as people expect. But it can also be lonely and difficult. Children are uprooted, family and friends left behind. Often, a spouses' hard-earned career must be put on hold. These are honest and important reports, which sketch both the highs and the lows of this peripatetic life. They are written engagingly and with the best of motives – to help others, by offering advice, encouragement and solidarity.

I offer my congratulations to all those who have contributed to this volume (authors and editor) and I warmly commend their stories.

Marina Wheeler, Queen's Counsel, is a writer and barrister practising from chambers in London. Appointed Queen's Counsel in 2016, she specialises in public and human rights law. She also teaches mediation and conflict resolution. Marina has recently written a historical family memoir, *The Lost Homestead*, based on the life of her Indian mother, who at one time worked for the Canadian High Commission in Delhi. Marina has four children and lives in east London.

Tiina Soini

Being a diplomat's spouse is truly being a Spouse of the World.

There is an old joke about a parent having to be everything from a cook to a referee. Multiply that by a trillion and that's a diplomatic spouse for you. The whole world is the third party in this relationship. Everything is accomplished with a serene approach and wise elegance, even during chaos.

The most important issue is not to lose your own identity. Holding on to your deepest inner world at all times, is the key. That is the tool you carry with you in all your roles as an individual, and also tasks for your loved ones and your country. Sustainable personal growth and developing coping skills are not only a normal narrative, but essential in surviving in changing environments and situations. Friends, companionships and peer groups are also fruitfully required.

Life happens to all of us. It doesn't necessarily wait for your next post in life.

We are privileged to share these intimate, intelligent and compassionate stories: *Spouses of the World*.

Tiina Soini
MD, Specialist in Psychiatry
Spouse of the former Party Leader 1997-2017, MP, MEP, Chairman of the Foreign Affairs Committee 2011-2015, Minister for Foreign Affairs of Finland 2015-2019, Mr Timo Soini.

Amanda Barton

All too often the voices of diplomatic spouses around the world go unheard. This anthology brings together, in a very personal way, their stories and experiences. We learn about the joys, challenges and difficulties of life away from home.

I have had the privilege to be both a diplomat and a diplomatic spouse. In my experience, it has been an unwritten rule that we are inclusive and take care of each other. I have met like-minded people who have become life-long friends. It is this sense of community that sustained and supported me through the challenges of life overseas.

The downside of this peripatetic lifestyle is, for me, never feeling fully settled anywhere. When I leave the UK, I miss my friends from home and when I return, I miss the friends I have made at post. And much as we have come to appreciate Zoom in the time of Covid-19, nothing quite makes up for personal contact.

On balance, I would not change a thing. Every posting has been an adventure and my time overseas has enriched my life.

Amanda Barton, spouse of Sir Philip Barton, the Permanent Under-Secretary of the Foreign, Commonwealth and Development Office, UK.

Jonathan Sweet

For many, the idea of travelling the world as the spouse or partner of a diplomat is an intoxicating one. The excitement of foreign travel; the chance truly to immerse oneself in the local culture – to get fully under the skin of what day-to-day life in Austria; Argentina or Australia is really like – the opportunity to forge friendships with other spouses and partners from across the globe; and, above all, the good fortune to do so while cosseted from some of the harsher realities by a privileged diplomatic lifestyle, sounds idyllic.

The chapters and stories in this book celebrate all of that and more but they also provide a valuable corrective to that one-sided perspective. They highlight the anxiety, stress and loneliness that so often accompany a move abroad as a diplomatic partner; the difficulty of sustaining an independent career; the transitory nature of friendships as other diplomatic spouses/partners move in and out of one's orbit; and the enormous strain that the diplomatic lifestyle can place on families, including children. Anyone who wants a proper understanding of what it's like to be a diplomatic partner in today's world should look no further than the profound, insightful and, above all, deeply personal experiences recounted here.

Jonathan Sweet
Executive Director, Diplomatic Service Families Association, Foreign, Commonwealth & Development Office, UK

Phil McAuliffe

We humans connect with each other through stories. And as people who live the diplomatic life, we know that there's power in sharing our stories with each other. Not only do we connect through these stories as people, but we also connect with others who know exactly what it's like to live this life.

The diplomatic life can be tough, and we all pay a price for living it. Sometimes, the price is one that we gladly pay, but others are those which we did not anticipate or did not think would ever happen to us, such as loneliness or disconnection through the loss of our own identity. This is what my work at The Lonely Diplomat is all about – creating a safe space to engage with the highs and the lows of this diplomatic life in a way that serves, supports, challenges and inspires you.

We can put enormous effort into making the difficult and the impossible look easy, but we know that this life can be anything but. Opportunities to share stories are opportunities to build real, authentic connection with others who we know really understand the highs and the lows of this diplomatic life. They must be seized. We who live this life are the only people who truly understand what it's like, and from this understanding this global community can be our own best source of support.

This book, and its stories, is one such opportunity.

Without doubt, you will see your experience reflected in some – or all – of the stories you're about to read. Sharing our stories to support others requires courage and vulnerability. Vulnerability is inspiring, and you may feel a special bond with the author. Please, if you read something that makes you laugh or pause and reflect, be sure to tell the author that their words, and sharing their wisdom and insight based on their experience, helped you. Don't miss the chance to connect!

Finally, the support structures around the global diplomatic community are evolving to reflect those who are accompanying diplomats. But this evolution is too slow. Too often, we don't see ourselves in the structure designed to support us. Exclusion based on position, title and gender is real. With more and more men accompanying their spouses on diplomatic postings, it saddens and frustrates me to see that there are still 'Diplomatic Wives Clubs' (read 'Wives of Ambassadors Clubs') in the world. We have a lot of work to do as a global community to ensure that there's diversity and inclusion, so that regardless of gender, sexuality or ethnicity, all feel that there's a place for them in the community should they wish to join.

Books like these can help start these important conversations within ourselves, with those around us and within the global diplomatic community. I want to commend all those involved in the writing, editing and collation of this book: the authentic connection that we all need can start here.

Phil McAuliffe
The Lonely Diplomat
www.thelonelydiplomat.com

Markku Keinänen

I was pleased to read these open and genuine accounts of all the challenges that spouses face regardless of whether you come from north or south, east or west. These challenges unite us all. A spouse or a child of a diplomat faces both sides of the proverbial diplomatic coin; there may be a high price to pay when travelling the world, but, on the other hand, the experiences gained, and friends made, enrich our lives in many ways.

My organisation (Ministry for Foreign Affairs in Finland) has worked hard for many years to improve the pension benefits for spouses, as well as general status of a diplomat's family. A lot has been accomplished but there is still more work to do.

The world is a better place when diplomacy works. Diplomacy works better when families are happy, and spouses bring their knowledge and expertise to our joint journey. I wish to convey my heartfelt thanks to all the spouses. Without you, there is no diplomacy.

Markku Keinänen,
Ambassador of Finland to UK (2019-2021), Permanent Representative of Finland to the European Union (2021-)

Janet Whitelaw Smith

This anthology is an engaging collection of anecdotal stories by spouses of diplomats from a wide variety of countries, which debunk the myth of the "crystal bubble" of diplomatic life. It explores the many challenges and experiences, both personal and functional, that spouses must contend with as expatriates. The diplomatic life is one of recurring dislocation and adaptation from the security of the known, belonging and established, to the challenge of the re-creation and maintenance of a safe and meaningful life in the different new. There are new languages and cultures to adapt to and function in; family members, possibly including children, to educate and nurture through the changes, and the constant rebuilding of a "home" and life. Career paths and income can be disrupted or lost. In many countries, experiences such as wars, civil disturbance, terrorist attacks, poor health and safety infrastructure, and the physical privations of food, services and materials have to be survived and managed in unfamiliar and even dangerous environments. This role must be achieved within the parameters of working within the representational expectations on a spouse in a diplomatic mission. Spouses of diplomats must develop the attributes of resilience, adaptability, self-reliance, empathy and, often, bravery to sustain their identity and independence, and to achieve fulfilment.

This well-written book chronicles the many achievements of spouses in this quest. It will be of interest to readers of biography and women's and gender studies. It is a must-read for anyone contemplating an expatriate life.

Janet Whitelaw Smith, spouse of former Australian Ambassador to the Peoples Republic of China and the Republic of Indonesia and Secretary of Defence, Richard Smith. Janet gained her BA in History and Biological Sciences from the University of Western Australia. While a senior high school science teacher, she married a fellow teacher who then joined the Australian Department of External Affairs in 1969. Their thirty-three years of overseas service began in 1970 in New Delhi, India followed by Tel Aviv, Manila, and Honolulu. The couple then went as Head of Mission to China and Mongolia, and to Indonesia. Janet taught in international schools in the first four of these postings and undertook voluntary charitable work in all the postings. Janet learnt four new languages and moved home twenty-two times. Following retirement in 2002, Janet became, and remains, a Voluntary Guide at the National Gallery of Australia specialising in Asian art and culture.

Mojca Stropnik

In life, the invisible often offers support and empowers the visible. Diplomats obtain a large part of their energy and communication power from their home environment, which is often veiled from others. An active, prudent and loving life partner in the centre of such an invisible world is a priceless support to the diplomat's demanding job. If they can both perform together at various events and gatherings in the visible world, they can greatly contribute to a successful accomplishment of the diplomat's mission.

Just as our complex world is better due to effective diplomacy, the diplomats are more successful when supported by their life partners and families.

I never shared the life of a professional diplomat and can only imagine the beauty, excitement and instructiveness of such life, on the one hand, but also renunciation, stress, moments of loneliness and constant learning, on the other. I came close to such experience when, as a life partner, I accompanied Dr Miro Cerar, Slovenia's former Prime Minister and later Minister of Foreign Affairs. I was offered the exceptional opportunity to meet presidents, prime ministers, ministers and diplomats, and spend time with their partners. There are many meetings that will stay in my memory. With the US First Lady Melania Trump, I engaged in a pleasant conversation in our native Slovene language. Within a short time, I witnessed Brigitte Macron's life energy and established a genuine contact with her. The friendly warmth of Amélie Derbaudrenghien, life partner of the former Belgian Prime Minister and current President of the European Council Charles Michel, will also linger in my memory. The extraordinary openness and friendly attitude of the Luxembourg Prime Minister Xavier Bettel and his partner Gauthier Destenay always put us in a good mood. Turkish President Erdoğan's spouse, Mrs. Emine Erdoğan, surprised me with her modesty and interesting topics of conversation. And I could go on and on.

However, despite the seemingly relaxed atmosphere, such meetings are also a challenge. One has to follow protocol rules, demonstrate general knowledge and promote one's country in the best possible way. A great part of all this takes place in front of the media, and any awkward behaviour or mistake is quickly noticed. When such public meetings, be it abroad or in Slovenia, ended, quietly and contentedly I used to step back into the sphere of the invisible, into the shelter of home, and continued to play the supporting role. I would take care of the family, go to work and do the usual daily chores. Miro was working day in, day out, and was often on business trips abroad. Another special challenge was the constant dealing with misinformation and media attacks that, through my partner or directly, also affected me and sometimes the whole family. Yet, all this was a priceless life experience. Many times, it was more bitter than sweet, but – in retrospect – undoubtedly gratifying.

The description of the visible and invisible aspects of the life and work of diplomats' life partners in this book is extremely telling. Among other things, it reveals the characteristics and sides of diplomatic life that we either do not know or do not understand well. The fact that the very people who experienced it talk about this life, makes this book even more convincingly authentic. All these stories and testimonies can be considered as a lesson and encouragement to anyone who is either already facing similar challenges or is preparing for them. At the same time, they are so genuine because of what they truly are: both life stories of individuals and stories of their co-existence.

Dear Spouses of the World,
Let me thank you for your contribution to the success of diplomacy – and to a better world for all. I wish you all the best.

Mojca Stropnik, life partner of Professor Miro Cerar – former Slovenian Prime Minister (2014-2018) and Minister of Foreign Affairs (2018-2020), is a lawyer and deputy president of the local electoral commission for national elections. Besides being involved in research projects on human rights and Slovenian constitutional development, she worked for the National Assembly of the Republic of Slovenia and was an expert advisor in the Office of the Prime Minister of the Republic of Slovenia. A successful athlete in her youth, she has remained active in sport as an IAAF athletic referee. She has one daughter, Maja.

Introduction

As a group, families of diplomats live a truly global life constantly on the move. Such a lifestyle can be incredibly rewarding and challenging at the same time. We change during this journey. Sometimes we may not be able to come back to where we started in one piece. We try to be culturally intelligent in all the countries we follow our diplomats to. Adjustments to each new posting should, in theory, be a piece of cake to us, but we are not sure whether there is any capacity for learning and accepting new thinking after the third, fourth or fifth country that we have lived in. Are we all trendy digital nomads who can keep our jobs while moving countries? Do we know how to help our children adapt swiftly to new homes but not become too attached to any place? What do we do now in a Covid-19 world when travelling is restricted?

Collectively, we reflect on these issues in this book. Most of us met in London in 2016. During the many meetings organized by Diplomatic Spouse Club London (DSCL), this book idea was born. We openly share our experiences, and we invite you to see us as we truly are.

Photograph: Margarita Mavromichalis, www.margaritamavromichalis.com

Section One:

At Post

Views on the city of Tegucigalpa, Honduras

1

My First Posting:
A Roller-Coaster Ride of Emotions

Amy Richardson

My husband and I had always dreamed of living overseas. As the wife of a newly minted diplomat, I looked forward to living in a foreign country, perfecting my Spanish, discovering a new culture, tasting new foods and meeting new people. We were assigned to Honduras for our first posting, and little did we know how difficult it would be.

We learned how unsafe the world can be when we took up our first posting. We moved from Ottawa, Canada to Tegucigalpa, Honduras: one of the most dangerous cities, with one of the highest homicide rates, in the world, according to the US State Department. Drug trafficking, gangs and gun violence rule that part of Central America otherwise known as 'El Triangulo del Norte' (the Northern Triangle), which is comprised of Guatemala, El Salvador and Honduras.

Looking back on it now, our first few months of living in Tegucigalpa were scary, to say the least. No amount of training could have prepared me for the constant awareness I needed simply to carry out the daily routine. Our compound comprised twenty homes on a dead-end street shared with an apartment block at one end. This gated community had two entrances, each patrolled by two men standing proud in their polished boots, and blue and grey uniform. A gun and extra bullets hung from a holster around their waists.

Inside the compound, our children – a toddler and an infant of four months when we arrived – played happily with the neighbours in the street, the small park and the shared pool, but outside those walls it was very different. Some of my neighbours had bullet-proof armoured vehicles and armed private drivers to shuttle them around town. I would lie awake at night visualizing violent scenarios where the children and I would get lost in a gang-controlled zone and be attacked, robbed at gun point, or worse.

We lived in a very large house in the gated community of Quinta Bella. The security measures included: armed and round-the-clock security guards, top-of-the-line alarm system, a bullet- and sound-proof room/ walk-in closet, reinforced triple-bolted doors, an elaborate emergency kit with food, medicine and water-sterilization tablets, personal panic button (which would immediately notify central command who would then send armed men to your location by motorbike), twelve-foot walls topped with barbed wire and eight (I counted them) electrified wires. Our first security briefing in Honduras was so alarming that I felt anxious and did not want to leave my house. A few days later, on our first attempt at a walk outside, the armed security guard at the gate of the compound raised his eyebrows and pointed to a mango tree a little over a block away and said, 'You must turn around there.'

When I did eventually venture out in the car, it was a whole new experience. There were very few street signs, making normal GPS navigation impossible. I ended up memorizing the basic safe routes. Driving in the city of Tegucigalpa felt like a real-life video game. Obstacles appeared, some of them whizzing in from odd directions with very little warning: stray dogs, cars reversing quickly on one-way streets, broken-down junk cars going ten kilometres per hour, large armoured vehicles speeding and weaving through traffic, grazing horses tied to the side of the road, motorcycles passing both on the left and right sides of the car, herds of cows crossing the street, overloaded trucks slowly chugging along the steep inclines, cars stopped and parked in the fast left lane. I quickly learned that the turn signal was more of a liability, a sign for drivers to speed up and *not* let me pass.

There was also the question of safety versus security. For example, when picking up my son from day-care, while painstakingly buckling him into his rear-facing car seat with its five-point safety harness, I would see one of his classmates clamber into the back of a bullet-proof vehicle driven by a personal chauffeur dressed in white shirt and red tie with an earpiece in one ear. The little boy would sit calmly beside his nanny, flanked by two armed soldiers in full camouflage uniform. (It turns out his father was a member of the local parliament.) In Canada, we have very strict rules regarding car-seat safety; in Honduras, the wealthy must protect themselves from possible kidnappings for ransom. Such contrast! My son is 'safe' in his car seat, but his companion is 'secure' from attack.

Once, during a period of political unrest, we drove past smouldering ashes and burning tyres spread across the road by protesters. We watched policemen extinguish the fire with buckets of water. At the time, I managed to stay calm and brush it off. This is how it is here in Honduras, I thought. We barely slowed down the car. It is amazing how our minds can rationalize these contradictions.

Just as I was starting to feel settled and comfortable with our new home, life sent us another challenge.

One month into our posting, and during our first family excursion, my husband had a major health crisis. That weekend, we were staying at a bed and breakfast in the countryside. Just as we were settling for an afternoon nap, my husband seized up, started moaning loudly, then turned blue and collapsed on the floor. He convulsed violently for several minutes as our children, wide-eyed, hid in a corner of the room. I panicked. Then adrenaline kicked in, and I screamed for help. The hotel staff came running to our rescue. Someone swept up my two young children and whisked them away from the chaos. I fumbled with our various government-issued cell phones, trying to locate the panic button. For several minutes (which felt like hours), my husband was incoherent, dazed and confused. A middle-aged, rough-looking man offered to drive us to the local clinic in the back of his pick-up truck. (He turned out to be the hotel's manager.) I was in a state of shock and panic as we bumped along the muddy gravel road back towards the rustic village we had passed mere hours before. My husband was still not able to talk coherently. He could not say his name clearly. At the tiny clinic, he slowly regained some awareness, and the young doctor urged us to go immediately to a hospital.

That is when we realized that the nearest hospital was three hours' drive through an extremely dangerous part of the country. Thankfully, it came to light that a colleague from the embassy was nearby and could drive us back to the capital. For the longest three hours of my life, we drove through the treacherous mountains in the dark, the children shrieking for food and attention as their parents stared worriedly out the window, imagining all the catastrophes that lurked in the shadows.

After several medical tests and more spontaneous, violent seizures, my husband was diagnosed. For a long time after that, I spent each day worried about a relapse, or worse, and could not leave him alone in the house. He insisted on continuing his work schedule. I was constantly afraid that another seizure might occur. The slightest bump or noise would take me back to that awful scene in flashbacks.

Meanwhile, life went on. I was still a mother and the spouse of a diplomat. Unfortunately, the political situation in the country worsened, and our safety situation reached a new climax.

Later that year, Honduras held presidential elections, the results of which were contested by both major parties. Because of the delay in proclaiming a winner and the uncertainty surrounding the electoral process, protesters took to the streets. These manifestations quickly turned violent as looters took advantage of the disorganization to spread chaos. The gangs capitalized on the unrest to settle their scores. The army and national police deployed in large numbers. The television news ran a constant loop of amateur videos showing people robbing department stores at gunpoint, looting banks, damaging gas stations, etc. One video showed a bank being swarmed as the tellers hid behind their desks, the armed guard helpless and cowering in his cubby.

Rumours began and often spread like wildfire over WhatsApp; friends and embassy staff passed on messages before verifying that the source of information was reliable. Our smartphones rang and vibrated constantly. I then filtered which messages to share, which messages were probably false and which messages I should pay attention to. This constant analysis of content was stressful. We were told to fill up our gas tanks and stock up on food just in case we needed to lockdown at home. Some days, I would hear loud bangs coming from outside our compound – were they daytime fireworks or gun shots? We were never quite sure. After dark, the city did not rest; we heard screeching sirens, beeping car horns, and chanting protesters in the distance, interspersed with the occasional gun shot or firecrackers. From our second-floor bedroom window, I watched soldiers just a block away pace to and fro as they monitored the traffic.

Amidst all of this, the children played on, oblivious to the disturbances. I sheltered them as best I could, but covering my anxiety with a calm mask took an enormous amount of energy. Meanwhile, my husband stayed busy with work and with testing effective treatments for his condition. I felt very alone. I continued to be trapped in our little gated community – no longer only in my mind but due to real security risks. The buses and taxis stopped running. The day-care was closed. My husband worked from home. I stopped making plans and play dates because we never knew which road protesters would block next. Things got so serious that we were asked to prepare an emergency carry-on bag with our essential belongings in case of an emergency evacuation. I wandered around our house aimlessly. How could I fit our whole life into one little backpack?

Eventually, the election results were announced, the soldiers went back to their barracks and we returned to life as usual. This type of heightened security event occurred several times during our two-year posting. We eventually got accustomed to seeing soldiers in fatigues hanging about, and the kids would even wave to them as we left the house.

I made friends with people whom I would not have initially expected to. For example, the 94-year-old woman who lived in the house across the street from us. Every afternoon, Nana would sit outside on an old sofa in the open garage of her home. I would often take the kids out to play in the street and then sit and chat with her. Now widowed, she came from a once wealthy and influential Honduran family. Despite the age difference, we quickly found several points in common: she had travelled all over the world, she spoke three languages and had been a primary school teacher – just like me! She narrated stories from her past and shared titbits and interesting facts about her home country. Since I was at home alone with a toddler and a newborn, it was a lifesaver to have these adult conversations to look forward to every day. Sadly, she died suddenly one Saturday afternoon. Her two maids came to us frantic, asking for help. We found Nana lying, grey and frail, in the living room, on the same sofa where my son often cuddled up with her to watch TV. We tried to contact her daughter, who was away at the time. Unfortunately, help did not arrive quickly enough. She passed away in transit to the hospital.

Thanks to my friendship with Nana, I am less shy when it comes to meeting new people. Whenever I was homesick, I looked at the empty sofa in the open garage across the street and instead of feeling sad I picked up the phone to call a friend back home or initiate a coffee date with a potential friend in Honduras. She taught me to treasure unexpected relationships.

We did make wonderful friendships and connections, including a young, single Canadian guy, a work colleague of my partner, who loved to spend Sundays hiking, swimming or simply baking with our family. We called these get-togethers 'Sunday Fundays' and they were often the highlight of my week. We also became friendly with a diplomatic couple from Colombia who invited us on their daily walks with their dog. We shared ad-hoc discussions on our front porch and lovely multicultural meals. We travelled together to the ruins of Copan (a world heritage site) and the little-known remote beaches in nearby El Salvador. We still keep in touch.

I connected with some people more easily and smoothly than with others. This had more to do with chemistry than social class, education, culture, language or background. These commonalities did help, but some of my richest exchanges were with individuals from very different backgrounds. The rotational aspect of overseas postings often meant that those people you made close connections with did not always stay around for very long, but returned to their home countries or moved on to postings in other parts of the world. I made a meaningful, close connection with a woman from Israel. She kindly introduced me to her group of friends called the *guapas cocineras* or 'pretty cooks'. This group of expat women met weekly to cook and chat together, exchanging recipes from their different cultures and backgrounds (Colombia, Costa Rica, Venezuela, etc.) and discussing their personal lives. They loved my chia pudding and now I get cravings for arepas (a cheese filled corn tortilla). Unfortunately, this group did not last very long; a few women moved away, and the delicate chemistry was lost.

In my neighbourhood, I rubbed shoulders with other diplomats, influential impresarios and political figures. A small, wealthy elite controlled nearly everything in the country from banks to grocery stores, construction companies and even politics. There was a huge gap between the haves and have-nots. I saw misery and poverty every time we left our house: children begging on the street corners, men and women sweeping the busy thoroughfares by hand amid the traffic nearby, disabled men begging for change, women peddling trinkets with their tiny babies strapped on their backs, barefoot children walking the street in search of garbage to salvage.

On a short trip to the grocery store, I might drive past people being chauffeured in their armoured SUVs and, at the stop light, find two little barefoot boys tapping on my window asking for a sip of my water and the rest of my half-eaten banana. Some days my heart sank, and I just wanted to burst into tears. Other days, I remained stone faced and looked straight ahead. What could I do alone? My diplomatic husband advised me to stay strong and treat everyone equally: it does not matter if you are the President of the Republic or the humble woman sweeping the road, you are human and you deserve to be treated with respect.

One day, our nanny Delmi asked if she could leave work an hour early. She explained that her cousin had given birth and needed help with the discharge papers so she could leave the hospital with her newborn baby. She was twenty-years-old and illiterate. Her partner was at work harvesting coffee beans in a rural village several hours away.

Having visited the hospital, and knowing the very high maternal and infant mortality rates in Honduras and for that establishment in particular[1], I had a very sad thought: I could have donated the clothes my daughter wore at twelve months and had outgrown, but the odds were that Delmi's cousin's baby might not live that long.

My previous visit was with a group of American expat wives. We donated small packs of diapers, baby wipes and pads to patients in the maternity ward. The conditions at this public hospital were, in one word, atrocious. The walls and ceiling were mouldy and crumbling down. There were no linens on the plastic hospital beds. There were several mothers to a bed, all lying in a stuffy windowless room. I observed new mothers walking around with huge towels between their legs to stem the bleeding. In the postpartum room, we counted maybe twenty women lying two to a cot with their babies perched precariously on the edges of the shared beds.

One doctor examined a woman as I handed out small packages of donated diapers. Smile. Congratulations. Stand in shock and want to run away as fast as I can from this intrusion on a private examination. As I turned to leave the room, the woman reached out and cried: '¿Y el mio?' ('And mine?') That little care package was not negligible to her. It felt like a tiny drop in the ocean to me. I received so much from friends and family, both in moral and physical support, when my children were born.

---

1. Website of the organization that coordinates the volunteers who help at the hospital (Fundacion Angelitos.) It includes statistics on the infant mortality rates: https://littleangelsofhonduras.org/

It was sometimes hard to see the positive when we saw such poverty around us every day. Some days, the differences – language, food, culture, and values – made me feel so alone and frustrated that I wanted to stay in bed with the curtains closed all day and not talk to anyone. Other days were filled with beautiful memories.

Here are a few examples, in no particular order:

- Greeting my 'Pineapple Man' at the weekly Friday market. He would always set aside the largest fresh pineapples for me: one for eating and one for making juice.

- At the Mayoreo Market, I made friends with farmers who encouraged me to taste new fruits and vegetables: papaya, guava, starfruit, passion fruit, yucca, plantain...

- We regularly make plato tipico at home. This is a traditional meal of refried black beans; rice; fried sweet plantain; tomato, onion and cilantro salsa; scrambled eggs and homemade corn tortillas. The children prefer this to pasta.

- Friday afternoon lunch dates for under twenty dollars with my husband. Thanks to our nanny and the embassy work schedule, we had exclusive time to connect as a couple on a regular basis over a delicious meal.

- Walking in the cloud forest in La Tigra National Park, surrounded by misty plants heavy with lush growth. The succulents on the trees provided water and food for the colourful birds and wildlife. We watched wild toucans playing in the trees. My daughter's first word for bird was 'guacamaya'. For a long time, she used the colourful parrot's complicated name for every bird she saw.

- Watching the sky light up with 360 degrees of artisanal fireworks during New Year's Eve celebrations in the city of Antigua, a UNESCO World Heritage Site in Guatemala.

- Snorkelling near the pristine coral reef off the beach by our bed-and-breakfast on the island of Roatan, Honduras. We had the place to ourselves and our children played in the sand under the coconuts. The cold snowy winters in Canada were but a memory as I watched from my hammock.

- Chartering a private plane with a group of twenty friends and family from Canada and Colombia. Together, we visited the beautiful ruins of Copan, Honduras. Early in the morning, we had the place to ourselves and felt like true explorers.

- During a trip to the beach in nearby San Salvador, we asked the waiter for some coconut milk. He pointed to the nearby palm tree and said, 'No problem!' Several hours later, after watching the fishermen bring in their catch on the beach, and some splashing in the refreshing pool, we still had not received our drinks. My son pointed to the palm tree and said, 'Mama, there is a man up in the tree.' Sure enough, the local Coconut Man was summoned just for us. He expertly climbed barefoot to the top of the tall tree. He carried a machete and a spray can (for the poisonous snakes) around his waist. Once he reached the bunch of lovely coconuts, he tied them to a rope, cut the stem and slowly lowered them down to the ground, where his assistant waited. We were each offered a refreshing green coconut and a straw with which to suck up the milk. Afterwards, the Coconut Man swung his machete again, this time to open the coconut so we could eat the delicious white pulp inside.

- Listening to my children playing with each other while talking exclusively in fluent Spanish.

- Time. Quality time with my children so I could give them my full attention and be in the moment.

- And the list goes on...

As a diplomat's wife, I lived in somewhat of a golden cage. We had a huge house, help in the home, a healthy travel budget and lots of free time, even though the security regulations restricted our freedom of movement and opportunities to explore our host country in depth. While the children learned fluent Spanish and we visited most countries in Central America, I struggled to find something meaningful to do with myself while on posting.

Then, I started writing my blog: adiplomatswifeblog.com. I wanted to paint the picture of what my daily life was really like. Writing let me work through my stress and cast off my negative emotions. When I wrote down a bad thought, it did not seem so bad after all, and the words on the page helped me put things in perspective.

Now that I am back in Canada, the whole two years spent in Honduras seems like a distant dream. The blog will keep the memories alive and be a good reminder for my children down the years.

Writing about our first posting has given me a sense of perspective. I came out of Tegucigalpa with the feeling of having survived with a capital S. This is the paradox of the golden cage: we lived the diplomatic lifestyle with all of its luxuries – but it wasn't always easy. Looking back, I am proud to say that I did it. I came out of it a much stronger and a wiser individual. I admit that I used the word adventure to romanticize for those back home what was an arduous journey full of ups and downs. I strove to see the positive in every hurdle and roadblock. If it was that hard for me – someone who had travelled before and who had the language and education to assimilate more easily – imagine how difficult it must be for the millions of refugees, undocumented migrants and immigrants who leave their homes and families for a new country in search of a better life.

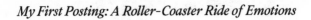

A beautiful phase in a chapter unfolds, treasuring these faces when the chapter folds.

2 Living in the Moment as a Professional Homemaker

Ratna Roshida Ab Razak

Involvement in the Foreign Service as a diplomatic wife has brought me new opportunities, along with a new profession and a tight schedule. In any one day, I need to fill many different roles, as if I am in a movie called *Life!* And I am playing all the parts. I will end up with a huge mess if I cannot juggle the mix of family duties, career obligations, educational responsibilities and travel arrangements. We, diplomatic spouses, are, to mention just a few of our positions, hostesses, chefs, employers (of domestic assistance), protocol specialists, event managers and students of international cultures and languages.

So far, I have lived in England (where I did my MA and PhD at Leeds University), in Japan (where my husband did his PhD) and again in England to support my husband's job at the Malaysian High Commission, where he works for Education Malaysia London, a department of student affairs. However, at home, I have a promising career of my own as a university lecturer at Universiti Putra Malaysia. When I realised I was not going to be able to work during my stint (spouses are very often hampered by visa constraints as well as family circumstances), I determined that my husband's posts might be the ideal time for me to get new qualifications, i.e., to become a competent homemaker and trailing spouse.

Although relocating spouses travel to numerous countries and enjoy all the highs and lows of cross-border, cross-cultural experiences, I do not think that the roles we play are so different from those of other women. For a woman, juggling several hats at the same time is not unique – there are wives who are homemakers and hostesses; working women who are members of professional societies and we are all partners in whatever our husbands need assistance with.

One has the extra responsibility of packing up and starting over many times as a diplomatic spouse. The positions one has developed must be dropped in one place and (perhaps) picked up in another. It can be disappointing and even cynical to someone who lives in such a way to stress the results of a long-term phase, such as a job.

We ought to live more in the moment. In this case, we need to strive to still be in a state of attention, a state of fullness of knowledge in the present and not living in the past, as well as thinking about the uncertain future.

I have found that living in the moment is the way around this topic: loving where I am, wherever I am; being conscious, alert and with all my senses in the present, not living in the past or thinking about the future. I try to make my soul happy because I truly believe that happiness is an option, and energy that we can develop daily. We need to do our utmost to live in high vibration energies like love, harmony, fun and joy for our well-being and satisfaction, and for the positive ripple effect it has on everyone around us and the whole world. Indeed, this is one of the most valuable life lessons I have acquired. I understand now how to live in the moment, or in mindfulness, since it carries tremendous benefits. I believe it is one of the essential keys to live a life that is secure, efficient, fulfilling and satisfying.

What I need to do is to concentrate my attention on the now and on the task at hand. This is important to make every day special, to feel positively about past activities I have given up, to have dreams for the future and to live fully in the present. I always remember this beautiful quote by Buddha, 'The secret of health for both mind and body is not to mourn for the past, worry about the future, or anticipate troubles, but to live in the present moment wisely and earnestly.'

As a Homemaker
I prefer to call myself a homemaker, not a housewife. For me, there is a contrast between a house that you can alter, only a building of bricks and mortar, stones and wood, and a home that includes several social, cultural, emotional and spiritual factors. A homemaker is someone who turns a house into a home.

The word housewife may be seen as an old-fashioned one that puts down women, implying that a woman is nothing more important than someone's 'wife,' only an unpaid girlfriend, and an assistant worker. I might be called a diplomatic husband's partner, which would take away my name and not remember any work I have done. Most wives, I think, particularly those who live in the diplomatic world, know how much work they do. If we are called domestic engineers, household administrators or children's development executives, we are dealing with many roles and several obligations.

It is not rare for trailing spouses to sacrifice their career or career aspirations during their trailing time. However, a common error in our perception is that sacrificing is long-suffering, which is frequently articulated in negative and uncreative ways.

This may be true at home, too. In my case, being a lecturer with a heavy workload, from Monday to Friday quality time as a family was limited to a few hours in the evenings, while my weekends and annual leave budget were normally reduced by the planning of lectures, marking student papers and assignments, and keeping up with my research progress.

Although I could say that I was passionate about my work, these commitments also needed to be paid off in terms of my family, my relationships and my health. It seemed that, for sacrificing my job, I was blessed with the possibility of enjoying life more. When something is done for the sake of God, in this case following my husband, it yields a personal well-being and spiritual fulfilment, and improves the quality of relationships.

To me, the role of the homemaker has become a spiritual practise of great significance for the future. Indeed, the home should be a place where both men and women, children and the elderly, all nationalities, creeds and abilities could be reconciled. Being a homemaker, however, forced me to do everything I needed to do at home because I really enjoyed it. Cooking, for example, turned into a work of art and a chance to delight all the senses. By cleaning, I have rendered the house – four walls and furniture – a place of warmth and comfort. By caring for the needs of family members, I have made the home a sanctuary for relaxation, a forum for conversation, a place for study and for sharing joys and sorrows.

To become a homemaker was to practise modern art – social art. To turn a house and everyone living in it into a home meant to create independence by opening a space where everyone is nourished. Homemaking has been both a spiritual and a practical application for me. Undoubtedly, the mission had its ups and downs, but the home was still the smallest culture, the microcosm of the macrocosm. Home renewal will bring a new social organism into being and affect the whole of society. It must, therefore, be based on a profound understanding of the mechanism that is involved both in the cosmos and in the individual forces of life.

Literature on child development proposes that the approach of children as active participants and members of society should start from the outset. On weekends or school holidays in London, it was my routine to take the children – I was blessed with four: Zafran (18), Zakuan (16), Zafira (14) and Zafrina (9) – to visit libraries, museums or other interesting places. It was an opportunity for our family to come together and have quality time in a special place, through an immersive learning experience that could provoke their imagination and deepen their curiosity.

While in London, I extended this focus outside the home itself to my children's school, where teachers often asked for parents to help. I love doing volunteer work; it has always made me very happy, and is a fun way to make friends in a new place. So far, I have helped school groups visit the Science Museum and Shakespeare's Globe Theatre. It is not how much money you have made that matters most to me at the end of the day. And you may be content with your job, but at the end of your career, you will need something new – something that needs you to find choices beforehand and to invest in friendships.

With all these events taking place throughout the week, quality time with family members has become a top priority for me over the weekends. Living just across from Hyde Park means there is no excuse for not being there, particularly on Sundays. Without a doubt, spending time together is a vital component of a successful marriage, and we found a nice way to do that on Sunday mornings. It is our routine to take a short walk and end up at a coffee shop. This gives us some uninterrupted time to catch up with life.

By not letting my identity as a trailing spouse hold me back and by choosing instead to take advantage of my privileges, I can be productive in focusing on my family and our home. I believe that whatever role you play, you need to be productive. Productivity is not about being busy, but about knowing when to have fun and when to work hard, when to relax and when to be serious, and making good choices every day, before the beneficial behaviours are reflected, and they become lifestyles. This is the only way to do tasks, such as laundry, dishes, sweeping up the house and organising family belongings. Planning family meals, creating shopping lists, buying groceries and preparing meals have become my core business as a homemaker. Since it is difficult to delegate these activities, I really wanted to be productive.

For me, efficiency can only be accomplished if it converges with resources and time. It is only when these three elements meet that the home can be managed efficiently. What I mean by time here is that, whatever the opportunity might be, you need to grab it and make the best of it. I formed a passion to carry out all the tasks and this stimulated me to achieve a higher level of competence.

The energy I put into being a homemaker was not limited to washing marks off walls or stirring pots. I learned the arts of the home and applied my creativity – the basic quality of a homemaker. According to Connie Fitzmartin in *Home with Fun: Ten Steps to Turn Your Home into A Fun Place to Live!* (2003), imagination can fix boredom and homemaking problems; my experience has led me to agree. For example, I finally found a workable solution to the awkwardness of disorganised closets, a system that I built myself. Indeed, imagination and ingenuity stimulated me to imagine scenarios, to make plans, and to see the outcomes of the planned acts before they were carried out.

As for time, you can see from the above that I have spent a large amount of time on homemaking. Below are some of the other things that I have devoted my time to, particularly in terms of developing in myself the qualities that I hoped would help me do a better job.

Being a homemaker, I need good judgement – an essential factor in all management activities and the consistency that allows me to be fair in responding to problems. Before taking a decision, I imagine, assess and analyse the problem and its solutions using my best judgement.

As a trailing diplomatic spouse, I could not earn an income, so my husband earned all our money. I had to use good judgement in buying decisions, while my husband was responsible for saving for retirement, a new home or family holiday. It was especially necessary to save for two people, not just one. This saving burden indicated that a substantial sum of money was taken from my husband's discretionary income per month, so I applied good judgement in budgeting to my other skills.

Perseverance, persistence, adaptability and self-management are also important essential attributes for all professionals. As a homemaker, I was confident that I could solve problems with these characteristics, however hard the circumstances I faced. For example, my children were attached to their friends in Malaysia, to the point that sometimes they would spend hours on phones, video games and social media. Face Timing was more exciting than their studies here. Informing and advising them constantly required me to be a persevering mother.

This has also been applied in directing their spiritual growth. Having faith in the Superpower, that is, God, really helped me to lead a fruitful lifestyle beyond the narrow and materialistic. However, as Sally Clarkson wrote in *The Mission of Motherhood* (2009), 'Our children will be tempted to stumble. No matter how vigilant our teaching, how welcoming our home, how profound our wisdom, our children will be tempted and must learn to grow their own faith'. As a mother who is full of God-consciousness, I need to preserve and maintain the life of my children's souls and spiritual expressions. I urged them to take care of the relationship between them and Heaven, such as through prayer, as well as the relationship with fellow human beings and nature. I did not stand still or give up my initiative, but I continued to do so until I had obtained the desired results, and gradually I was able to identify the challenges and find ways to solve them.

Adaptability meant versatility in adjusting to various situations, introducing new approaches and adapting to new circumstances: the basic attribute of a diplomatic spouse. To get the most out of living at a post, I needed to get out of my comfort zone, to adapt to a new life and to new people with a new culture.

It is not always as easy as it would seem to fit in with life abroad. But living in London, the metropolis that cherishes every nation and ethnicity, made it easy for me, particularly during the transition from living as a foreigner to a more local lifestyle. London helps anyone to follow their own culture.

Self-management is particularly important since hosting visitors, a long staple of diplomacy, requires stamina. I have always told myself that I needed vitality, good health and physical strength to carry out my duties. I had to schedule my job, provide rest times, and use task-simplification strategies to prevent needless exhaustion, but then resourcefulness is the hallmark of homemakers.

Being a diplomatic spouse has improved my ability to manage and use resources in the best possible way. For example, when important visitors are coming, and you only have three hours to settle everything! This happened when my husband told me that there was a group of five people from the Ministry of Higher Education, Malaysia, coming to have dinner at home.

The issues involved in setting up the foundation of a new life certainly include rediscovering and redefining the meaning, purpose and value of certain accompanying spouses; in that sense, retaining an identity is part of self-management. I believe that, as Viktor Frankl says in *Man's Search for Meaning* (1946), 'As every circumstance in life poses a challenge to man and poses a dilemma for him to solve, the issue of the meaning of life can actually be reversed. At the end of the day, man should not ask what the purpose of his life is, but must understand that it is he who is asking.'

Some people do not consider homemaking as a worthy activity. But for me, after the first two years of unpaid leave from my professional job, I firmly believe that remaining at home and taking care of my family should be valued and considered a career option.

Marie Kondo, in *The Life-Changing Magic of Tidying* (2014) says, 'Home is the place where we appreciate all the items that help us. It's where we're going to review and reconsider ourselves. It is therefore very important to make our home full of positive vibrations and a beautiful environment that can represent our real life.'

Being a full-time housewife has given me a golden opportunity to make a home comfortable, happy and safe, with fun memories that my family will remember fondly. In his book *The Dream Society* (2001), Rolf Jensen points out that while people are getting richer, they are always searching for spiritual elements or goods in order to provide a good living atmosphere. So, it was my duty to provide decorations that represented splendour and elegance, that were emotionally and spiritually engaging, and also rich in story and meaning with emotional impact.

In order to make my new location in this foreign country my new home, I took along some of the things that I love. It was not difficult in terms of finances since the Malaysian government provided us with shipping and relocation allowances. So, I took items like my favourite piece of art, some chinaware, books, bookshelves, and so on. With something familiar to hold on to, my settlement phase has been easier than expected.

In reality, thank God, I have not had trouble adapting to new cultures. Some of my friends, though, have told me that moving has led them to wonder about their identities and be severely unhappy. Perhaps my interest in meeting people, my own skill set, and my personality made a difference. In addition, enthusiasm, openness to learning and forming friendships, and a sense of humour, helped. Indeed, learning to live in a moment was a key, an approach that helped me to embrace my identity as a diplomatic spouse with joy, purpose and passion. To me, the benefits of being a professional homemaker turned out to be much greater than the losses.

As an Academic on Leave

While I have to put my career on hold to help and manage my companion's posts abroad, I have been fortunate to be posted to London. Being in London was something to be grateful for as an academic who was still doing research, since I had the opportunity to find references in many libraries, particularly the collections of the School of Oriental and African Studies (SOAS) at the University of London, the British Library and those of Oxford and Cambridge Universities outside the city.

One of my favourite things in London has been attending talks and lectures from respected speakers, such as Professor Tariq Ramadan of St Antony's College, Oxford, who teaches contemporary Islamic studies at the Faculty of Theology and Religion, and the Faculty of Oriental Studies.

In this way, I kept up with my original career. When my husband was posted to the United Kingdom, I was asked to play an adjunct role. I have temporarily moved from university to the Foreign Service – a body of working professionals dedicated to serving Malaysia's interests in the field of education and caring for the needs of Malaysian students. The purpose of my husband's position, and therefore of my adjunct role also, was to create friendships internationally, and to promote networking between Malaysian and worldwide higher education institutions.

Unlike my husband, I did not have an official job description as a diplomat's wife. It was indeed a derivative status and an ambiguous position, but the spouses of those serving in the Ministry of Foreign Affairs were, without doubt, non-official representatives of Malaysia. We were all supposed to be smart conversationalists, well-versed in local and foreign affairs.

In spite of these obstacles, my message to all prospective diplomatic spouses is to keep their heads high.

As a Hostess

When I took on the role of diplomatic wife, being a not very well-trained cook gave me the wonderful experience of learning. Part of my main business, a staple of the so-called diplomatic life, was to entertain visitors.

From the very beginning, we were told that a wife who was an experienced hostess was important to diplomatic objectives. The talent of a wife will help to promote bilateral ties between countries. It was enjoyable for me to host visitors, but it was quite exhausting because I usually took a couple of hours to set up everything.

I enjoyed entertaining people in our home and welcomed more than a hundred groups over a span of almost two years, mostly because I am such a homebody. I did not mind putting in the work if I had to do it from my home. I find hosting rewarding, from the early planning to the end of the event. For all that I knew about manners, ingredients and general dining style, I owed thanks to my mum, and personal trial and error, but I still found my own flare for my dinner parties. One of my favourite ways to celebrate a significant occasion, particularly with all our families, especially in London, was to get a bunch of people over for a festival like Hari Raya (the Day of Celebration, which marks the end of Ramadan for Muslims).

To make sure that every event is unforgettable for my guests, I start with the intention of making it so for God's sake. In a comfortable and wonderful environment full of good vibes, welcoming visitors is all about enjoying fun and joy that puts everyone, including the host, at ease.

We believe, in Malay culture, that welcoming visitors into our homes is welcoming riches, so we need to handle our visitors very well. Having visitors at our home in London was an opportunity to introduce foreigners to Malaysian culture, so, I had to do my best. Normally, I would decide which main course and dessert I wanted to prepare when my husband told me there were visitors arriving. Then, I would clean the whole house, especially the places where visitors went, such as the dining room, the living room and the bathroom, and ensure that the garbage bin and the dishwasher were empty. I love flowers, so I would buy some and place them in vases.

I did all this on my own because I did not have a chef or a maid. It was challenging often, but I took it as an opportunity to test my stamina and perseverance in managing several items.

This is how an evening at home might look to a visitor who does not know Malaysian culture: I deliver a drink to the guests, usually juice, when they arrive. There are typically three courses. After that, I serve coffee or tea, and occasionally *Teh* (Tea) *Tarik* (Pulling), a very special Malay tea. Usually, we drink it at the coffee table in the living room. I do not divide men and women. They eat the same things at the same time and place. Often, I cannot sit with the guests because I am too busy running up and down to the kitchen.

If our guest is coming for lunch or dinner, and I wish to serve Malaya cuisine, (a cooking tradition of Malayan ethnicity) – first, I would ask if they were all right with the idea. I could shop in Chinatown (near Charing Cross Road) for food from Malaysia, or in Wing Yip, a local Chinese supermarket, offering a wide range of *Tean's* Gourmet and *Brahim*, two popular Malaysian gourmet brands.

As for etiquette, aside from what I learned from my mother and the Malaysian Diplomatic Spouse Association, PERWAKILAN, the travel guides published by *Lonely Planet* provided me with a lot of knowledge about international brands, customs and protocols.

To be a good diplomatic spouse, you need to be the best version of yourself. Always keep in mind that people should not forget how we make them feel. As the Golden Rule says, 'Do to others as you want others to do to you,' so this should be your essential rule.

Without a doubt, the job of the diplomatic spouse is, above all, to serve her country. That is why I tried my best to invite my friends to come to my house, so I could introduce Malaysia better. It was a great job for me that came with great honour as well as great responsibility; I was at the post to build a positive and desirable picture of my home country and to educate the diplomatic and local community about the different aspects of life in my country.

As a Member of PERWAKILAN

The Malaysian Ministry of Foreign Affairs Ladies Association, also known as PERWAKILAN, which all Malaysian diplomatic spouses are expected to join, is very significant. Its primary goal is to provide participants with the opportunity to meet, share knowledge and encourage others to settle down and adapt to their new environment. It is also a forum for participants to provide support to the less fortunate through their voluntary work and events.

The goal of the association is to assist new members with knowledge, such as on the etiquette, customs and traditions of Malaysia and the host country. PERWAKILAN also cooperates from time to time with other women's voluntary organisations and individuals to further the goals of the association, through exhibitions or receptions offering opportunities to promote Malaysian culture and food.

PERWAKILAN carried out a variety of activities that demanded the full support and participation of all the ladies in the community. This was a golden opportunity for me. As the association's secretary for two years, I have given it my full devotion.

As a Malaysian Community Member

As the spouse of a Malaysian diplomat in London, I felt obliged to know about fellow Malaysians living in my host country, whether they were students, members of local communities, or short- or long-term tourists. The Malaysian community in the United Kingdom is massive. A survey conducted by the International Organization for Migration reported that approximately 180,000 Malaysians were living, working or studying in the United Kingdom in 2007. The largest number of Malaysians in the United Kingdom was 48,000 in London, followed by Manchester, Birmingham, Sheffield and Leeds. Due to this large population, there are many Malaysian food shops open, particularly in big cities. This represents Malaysians' passion for good food!

Makan Café, Malaysian Deli and Tuk Din are among my favourites. Having a good relationship with the owners gave me a great opportunity to better understand life in London. What better way to get in touch with other Malaysians, if not over delicious food at authentic Malaysian restaurants? And because of the great atmosphere in these businesses, I enjoyed bringing my non-Malaysian friends there to support Malaysian cuisine and music. London is always buzzing with great events and festivals. Puan Fatimah Gammage, a resident here for almost thirty years, was a good source of information. She loved to invite me to interesting programmes, especially when they were about music, fashion, dance, arts, crafts and food, and also to enjoy her beautiful and serene garden.

As a City Explorer and Traveller

As a diplomatic spouse and, at the same time, as an academic researcher, I intend to write a book or at least a short academic article about my experiences. To do so, I need to participate in more diplomatic activities and meet more diplomatic spouses. At the same time, I must explore the host nation and learn about its history, culture, heritage, customs, values, business leaders, etcetera. I must learn at least the basics of the language, too.

Living abroad has given me a chance to move slowly and get to know my host country as a local. No more attempts to compress a lot of sightseeing in the few days that I would have as a tourist – instead, my family and I spend weekends exploring museums, historic sights and natural wonders at our leisure and revisiting them time and time again.

Living in a country with four seasons is not new to me. However, in any season, the UK can still give me a lot of things to do. In my hometown in Malaysia, we have just one season – summer – that is hot and wet all year round. There is something unique about each of the English seasons. It is popular for English people to think of spring as a time of birth and a new beginning. However, as a Malaysian who is used to only one type of weather, this was a new experience. I enjoyed searching for the sweet yellow and orange shades of the daffodils; to venture into gardens and parks searching for tulips, roses, and rhododendrons in their seasons. London might be a huge metropolis, but it has a lot of hidden pockets of green space. I also enjoyed visiting libraries and second-hand book shops and exploring historic buildings such as Kenwood House and Knebworth House, places that provided me with great knowledge on the history of London and the United Kingdom through a selection of historical manuscripts.

Based on my three years of meaningful life as a diplomatic spouse, I advise every diplomatic spouse to pay complete attention to what you do and to seize every moment of life. This is vital because it will allow you to prolong its sense and importance, and make your temporary life a meaningful one. Go out and explore; it will give you moments of joy and opportunities to serve your country. The chance to be in this country could come one day. So, make the most of your time, catch all the beautiful moments, build all wonderful memories, and do not forget to spread your affection, love, compassion and positive vibes.

I do hope that those who have the same life experiences, challenges and thought processes try their best to make each day count. Do become more mindful to appreciate, value and cherish every single moment of your life and grab everything you possibly can. This is because mindfulness itself is actually the fuel and energy by making us awaken to utilise the present moment in the best way possible. Thus, it is up to us whether to enjoy each moment of each day or let it go with the wind. Always ask yourself what in the future, especially when you are in your home country, you want to look back and smile at. As a piece of advice, never consider the chance of becoming a diplomatic spouse to be a loss or a missed opportunity. Opt for this role with wide-open eyes, and it will be clear that it is not a downgrade; it is just another, new, existence.

The most significant change that happened to me while I was a diplomatic spouse was in my personal development, which took several forms. I became more independent when, without the immediate help of my family and friends from home, I began to learn how to do things on my own. Since I spent a lot of time by myself, I learned to respect myself, to discover things that I really loved, and to see my work-life balance differently. All these different aspects of life helped me to live in moments as a happy and productive homemaker, a goal-oriented on-leave educator, as well as a gracious and humble hostess.

Being a diplomatic spouse also meant that I had the opportunity to travel to places that I may have dreamed of and to meet fascinating people from a range of backgrounds, cultures, customs and ways of thinking. Forming new friendships became second nature when I lived in a new country. It was very important to my well-being, and it made me feel as if I could not survive without friends. I am unbelievably grateful for the wonderful people I met in London. Indeed, the experience I have gained from being a diplomatic spouse has made me a stronger person.

I have found diplomatic and charitable events to be gateways to non-Malaysians, to get to know us well, particularly our fashion, music and culture. I have been in a unique position to help promote the cultural highlights of my country, especially our national dress, cuisine, music, literature and visual arts.

Indeed, this is a very wonderful experience, and one that I will treasure forever.

Kiss by a giraffe in Kenya

3 Pregnancy, Birth and Motherhood

Nina Rousu

When I was asked to write about being a diplomatic spouse, I knew my story would have to cover the most important year of my life: the year I became a mother while on diplomatic posting. It is hard to say to what extent the events that took place and the emotions I felt had to do with motherhood and how much of it had to do with it happening on post; I have never been pregnant or given birth anywhere else, so I have no point of comparison. By the time I was ready for a child, I had been living abroad for several years. I had missed the births and baby years of my nephews and nieces and all the pregnancies of my best friends back in Finland. I had no idea what to expect. I just knew that I wanted to be a mother and I had been told it is 'the most natural process,' so I went into it thinking it would be fairly straightforward despite our situation.

Whatever the diplomatic life throws at me, I always like to write things down afterwards and, with the help of afterthought, to try to see the humour in even the most bizarre and stressful of events. Perhaps that is how I manage my own mental health. Do not get me wrong – I am fully aware that my life is incredibly easy and privileged, and that is why, rather than complain, I prefer to laugh at it. In the end, I love this lifestyle and feel as if I was made for it. With all its uncertainty and temporary chaos – whether I am doing something as life changing as giving birth or as everyday as buying milk – there is always an adventure to be had, and I would not have it any other way. These adventures are what I want to remember when I am old, and I hope to laugh at all of them.

My partner and I were both in our early thirties when we arrived for our first posting together and decided it was time to start a family. We had gathered it was not an easy task, and it could take months, even years, if we were so lucky as to become parents at all. Just a couple of weeks later we were pregnant, and a bit shocked. We had thought we would have much more time to prepare, both mentally and with respect to practicalities. Uganda, where we were posted, was a medical evacuation post, which meant that beyond routine GP appointments, our insurance company did not recommend that we have any medical treatment there. This brought with it some logistical challenges.

For me, first-time pregnancy was a confusing period, and living far away from family and friends made it even more so. Every posting is different, every pregnancy and birth is different, every baby is different, every mother, too. Let me take you on my journey into motherhood. I invite you to learn from my mistakes, for I made many.

'Now you can start to exercise your uterus every day by holding your breath for 20 minutes.'

I was seven months pregnant with my first baby. I had to blink a couple of times as the advice was sinking in.

'Do you mean my stomach muscles?'

'Yes.'

At that stage of my pregnancy, I was unable to hold a thought for 20 minutes, let alone anything else, so I decided not to discuss the exercise any further.

'Now you can do *susu*?'

I had already worked out that this was the Luganda word for a urine sample. I withdrew my full figure to the little toilet booth with a small plastic drinking cup I had picked up from the water dispenser earlier; it doubled as a sample dish.

Our first visit to the local surgery had taken place around the eight-week scan. As first-time parents, we simply could not wait until the twelve-week scan, which is what our insurance covered, and decided to pay for one ourselves to have a quick peek. I was very nervous, and I wanted to know everything was as it should be.

We arrived at the surgery reception only to be guided right back out the door to the back of the plot towards a shed that looked like it could house a lawnmower and other garden tools, rather than ultrasound equipment. However, in that little garden shed we got to see a little pulsating bean that was going to be our baby, and discovered that all was as it should be. Afterwards, we were given a hand-written report that stated: 'Expected due date 8th August 2009'. All well, except that the date of the scan was July 2008 and the report suggested I would be pregnant for 14 months! Perhaps a slight miscalculation or just a typo, but we were sure we would find out the actual due date eventually.

I was lucky in that my friend, who knew exactly how clueless I was, sent me a rough guide to pregnancy, one that did not list all the things that could go wrong (and there are so many, I discovered online!) but that gave me the sound advice I needed amidst all the interesting advice I got from my young Ugandan midwife. I think she was new in the job and I was her first mzungu (non-African) client. She was probably not used to a patient who Googled every piece of advice she sagely offered, and it certainly did not help that English was the second language for both of us. Often, her Luganda English and my Finnglish passed each other by; we simply could not understand each other. She certainly tried her best and was always very thorough, helpful and kind, and, despite some misunderstandings, she was able to monitor my pregnancy just fine.

Sometimes, the confusion was more a matter of equipment malfunction. Around the middle of my pregnancy, I climbed once again onto the scales, and the midwife screamed, with clear panic in her voice, 'You have lost five kilograms!'

Calmly, I gazed down at my mountainous figure. I had not seen my toes in weeks.

'That sounds like a lot, I sincerely don't think I have. Could you check again?'

It turned out the scale had not been calibrated, and after three tries and adjustments we got to a figure my midwife could be happy with. However, I still was not entirely sure what my actual weight was, and because everything made me nervous, I bought some digital scales and decided to keep an eye on my weight gain myself. Just in case.

To make sure that I kept gaining weight, I was told I should maintain a healthy diet. Helpfully, the surgery had prepared some printed advice on what to eat during pregnancy. 'It is important to make sure you get enough protein in your diet,' it said. 'If you are vegetarian it is easy to get protein. Just add meat to your normal vegetarian dishes, like stews, pasta and rice.' I found most of this quite entertaining, and thanks to our internet connection I was able to find answers to all my questions about pregnancy diet on my own. Mind you, I did not have much of an appetite, as I suffered from a severe case of morning sickness through the day, every day, throughout my whole pregnancy.

On one occasion, the vomiting just would not stop and I was so dehydrated I had to go to the surgery, where I lay semi-conscious on a drip. I was given medicine, blue pills, which I took without questioning. I stopped vomiting, but I was out cold for the next 24 hours. My husband had to keep waking me up to eat and drink, propping me up against pillows and slapping me on the cheek to keep me awake between spoonfuls of soup. Two days later, at a check-up, I told the doctor I could not feel my baby move, and he just said, 'The baby is asleep, the medicine can make you a little drowsy.' I was quite upset. If I had known that the medicine would affect my baby, I would not have accepted it. I learned a valuable lesson: to ask about possible side effects *before* taking any medication, since very little information was ever volunteered.

Very soon after my hospitalisation, I had an extremely vivid dream. I was back home in Finland, in my favourite pick-and-mix sweets store, running through the aisles of sugary treats, filling up a large bag with all of my favourites. I went to the cashier, paid, and as soon as I was out the door, I opened the bag, ready for a feast. To my disappointment, I pulled out fresh berries instead of sweets. I woke up and knew I had to have Finnish sweets. I had been so unwell, this was my first craving, and I had no choice but to obey it. I even believed the sweets would help with the nausea.

I believe, when women have pregnancy cravings, they traditionally wake up their husbands in the middle of the night and send them out to get what they need. This was not an option for me. But I did manage to find an online store that sold Finnish sweets for a hefty profit, and I quickly proceeded to order more than £100 worth. I asked for delivery via Her Majesty's diplomatic post, known as the Diplomatic Bag. Two weeks later, I got an email saying the Foreign Office bag room had confiscated my sweets, as food was not allowed in parcels. I had not realised. I tried to argue that this was not food but medication, to no avail. I had to wait another three weeks for my husband to travel to London for work, and finally, on his return, I got my fix. I cried when I opened the first bag of salty liquorice laced with ammonium chloride. (Yes, Finns love this stuff.) Unfortunately, it did not stop me from vomiting, but finally I could eat something without gagging.

Because we were sent on a posting by Britain's Foreign, Commonwealth and Development Office (FCDO), I was entitled to the same care that the NHS provides back in the UK. That is why I received an NHS maternity package through the same diplomatic post. I have seen the famous Finnish baby box every new mother gets in my homeland; unfortunately, the British version did not come close. The Finnish box includes all the essential clothes for the newborn, a mattress that fits the box so there is no need for an expensive Moses basket, nappies and other useful things. The British box mainly has adverts: for formula, nappies, baby powder – everything money can buy. I went through the piles of adverts trying to find something useful. Finally, on the bottom of the box, I found a small pregnancy calendar. It came with colourful stickers you could attach on relevant days, with exclamations like: 'Can't see my toes today!' and 'Bellybutton out!' I sat on the floor next to the pile of adverts and covered my face in my hands. I had just realised how old I must be for a first-time mother. It had been decades since I was attaching colourful stickers to a calendar! The one thought that had been growing in my mind throughout my 'throw-up pregnancy' was *Never again!* and, surprisingly, there was no pink sticker for that.

At the regular check-ups, my midwife kept feeling my belly and telling me my baby was breech. I was worried about everything at that stage, especially anything that might complicate the delivery, so I quickly marched in for another scan in the garden shed to find out that my baby was actually head down and, judging from the familiar kicks he delivered to my diaphragm, he had been that way for a while. This may have explained why the midwife could never find the baby's heartbeat – she was looking in the wrong place. I was pretty worried in the beginning about the missing heartbeat, but she explained to me, 'He is just moving around so much I cannot catch him.'

There were a couple of things my midwife was very right about. She told me one day, 'This baby will be early, because the first baby is always early.'

I had heard a very different statistic and said, 'I thought it was other way around and the first one is often late?'

'No, no, the first one is always born early but the labour is very long and painful!'

She also told me, 'You will not push, because you are only small.' I dismissed this information as a misunderstanding and once again relied on Google. There is, of course, an abundance of online chat groups and blogs that can scar you for life, but there are also very helpful resources, like the NHS website. The trouble was that some of the advice was different in different countries, and I was trying to balance between at least three. It would have been easier to pick one country and stick to it.

To prepare for birth and parenting, my husband and I enrolled ourselves on a Lamaze birthing course, held by one of the American expat ladies in our neighbourhood. There, we discussed the different stages of giving birth, learned to bathe a doll with imaginary soap and water and mastered the all-important swaddling techniques. I had read most of these things by now in my many pregnancy books, but still it felt comforting, practicing the skills in a group and seeing that other first-time mums were just as uncertain as I was about what to do with the baby when it arrived. More than anything, the birthing course was a nice chance to meet other parents-to-be. After a brief chat, it was clear we were all equally lost, and that somehow, at that stage, was how it was meant to be.

Soon enough, I was eight months pregnant and ready to travel away for 'confinement' – an unusually stuffy term, which sounded rather penal to my foreigner's ears. Although an average Ugandan woman gives birth to six to seven children in her lifetime, my insurance company offered me UK and South Africa as my official confinement destinations. I could also opt for Finland, but then I would have to organise medical care and all the practicalities myself while still in Uganda. I was happy to conform and went with South Africa, our closest medical evacuation country. My due date had by now been brought forward from August to March, and I had heard it is a lovely time of year to be in Cape Town. I had no idea of the enormity of things I was deciding on, and I based my decisions mainly on the practicality of not having any winter clothes for myself or the baby, which ruled out the UK and Finland.

Instead, we made this brief birthing plan: a few weeks of holidaying in sunny Cape Town with friends, then my husband would join me. I would give birth. He would stay for two weeks of paternity leave followed by a week of summer holiday, then he would return to Uganda and I would follow as soon as I could. The plan seemed to work really well on paper.

It was only later, when I was packing my bags with muslin squares, dummies and a breast pump that it started to dawn on me that this was no regular holiday. I suddenly understood I was going to come back with an actual, real human baby, who would then stay with us for the next who-knows-how-many years. I closed my suitcase and knew there was no turning back: I was going to travel into motherhood.

I arrived in Cape Town and found myself an obstetrician and a hospital. My friend Helen, who happened to be on holiday, joined me from the UK to keep me company while my husband was still in Uganda. We wanted to aim my husband's short paternity leave as close to the birth as possible so that the new dad could spend some time with his baby. Of course, we knew births are notoriously unpredictable, but thanks to Dr Google we were hopeful nothing would happen much before the due date.

I was determined to make the most of my last ever child-free holiday, so on a beautiful Wednesday morning Helen and I joined a bus tour around Cape Town, then had a wonderful meal overlooking the sea in Camps Bay, and as the sun was slowly setting, we walked barefoot on the beach. What a lovely day.

Poor Helen, her sunny holiday was cruelly interrupted the next night with the classic: 'Wake up, I think my water just broke!'

I had had no warning, nothing. *Hold on! This is not at all how I planned it*, I thought. It was still two full weeks to my due date, and my husband was meant to arrive in Cape Town the following evening, but my body had another plan.

I had been so sure of not going into labour any time soon, I did not even have my hospital bag packed, so in blind panic I threw some random – and it later turned out, totally useless – things in my overnight bag and we headed to the hospital. Just before we locked the door to our flat, Helen turned back and got her camera, just in case. I was already wobbling down the stairs, still hoping against all odds this was a false alarm.

I put a towel on my seat and drove us to the hospital in my rental car through the empty, dark streets of Cape Town. I was scared, confused and in some pain, but I had no choice: I had to focus enough to drive. Calling a taxi in the middle of the night was not considered safe practice in Cape Town, and I reasoned that, since Helen was not registered to drive our rental car and did not know her way around Cape Town, this was the only way. In hindsight, I should have let her drive, of course, but let us just say I was not thinking straight. I parked in the hospital car park and tottered in.

It did not take long for the nurses to determine that I was in labour and they rushed to call and wake up my doctor. Helen wisely asked if we should call my husband. It had not even occurred to me. I must have been in shock. I called him on my mobile, and far away, in our bedroom in Uganda, he answered and sounded very sleepy. He was due to catch his first flight towards Cape Town early that same morning. I explained the situation and told him that I would keep him posted through the night.

My doctor soon appeared at my bedside. She read the charts and confirmed my baby was on his way. Helen had to step in for my husband, to hold my hand and keep me company all night. I was so lucky to have her around; I would have been absolutely terrified going through it all alone. At least I had one familiar face among all the strangers. And so, it turned out that, although my baby was not breech, I did end up going into labour two weeks early and having a C-section, just as my Ugandan midwife predicted. Helen had to don scrubs, and her holiday photo album took a rather unexpected turn when the paediatrician grabbed her camera and snapped some close ups of my belly being cut open and my baby emerging into the world.

All went well in the end, if not entirely according to our birthing plan, and our son was born healthy and lovely. I held him, not quite believing what had happened, scared that I might break him, all my instincts telling me one thing: protect.

A couple of hours later, my husband caught a plane from Entebbe to Fatherhood. By the time he arrived, our son was all clean and rosy cheeked and swaddled up, and I lay, slightly frazzled but already oblivious to the chaos of the previous night, in a clean hospital bed, my window overlooking Table Mountain. My husband missed the birth, but it seemed like a minor detail when, after a day of flying, he finally arrived at the hospital and got to hold his son.

My husband's paternity leave was a haze of wakeups, feeds and nappies, and over way too quickly. By then, I felt so overwhelmed I decided I should not be trusted alone with a newborn, so I called in my mum, who flew all the way from Helsinki to Cape Town to help me with our imminent move back to Uganda.

First, our baby needed a passport and a visa. For the passport, we needed his hospital birth certificate to be approved and stamped by a local government office. So, we queued with our newborn all day in sweltering heat to prove that he was, in fact, born, and that we were his parents. Then, we needed to queue at another office to get an apostille for the notarised document. We were then able to apply for my son's British passport at the embassy. But first, we needed a passport picture.

Getting a passport photo taken might seem like a very trivial detail, but the whole process took us more than an hour. The rules are rather strict: eyes must be open, parents cannot be visible in the photo, and somehow, without any neck muscles, the head has to be straight, and the baby has to fully face the camera. First, I placed my baby on the shop floor on a white towel and the photographer straddled him, waiting for him to open his eyes. He did no such thing. At that age, most babies sleep more than 20 hours a day. I tried to pick him up, undressed him, made noise, even shook him slightly and, finally, he squinted just long enough for the photographer to capture the most hideous photo of a newborn ever taken. My beautiful baby looked so downright ugly and ridiculous in the photo, guards at every border post laughed aloud at his passport photo for the next five years.

In the end, I managed to get him a passport, a visa, all relevant vaccinations and an all-clear from his paediatrician. My baby was ready to travel. My doctor, on the other hand, was a bit doubtful. 'Do you really have to leave already? It's been only six weeks and you had a major operation. You should rest.' But I was running on postpartum hormones and I just wanted to go home and be with my husband, to return to normality. Thinking back now, it might have been a much better idea to just lie down for a couple of weeks.

Packing was a nightmare, and, thankfully, my mother was there to help. The FCDO allowed us a small shipment for our baby things as not much was available in Uganda. Quickly, we had to do all the shopping for the whole first year of my baby's life and hope we got it right. We then had to pack it all securely and get it picked up from the flat. This coincided with my son deciding he wanted to feed through the day and night at twenty-minute intervals. I felt all the energy being sucked out of me but still I had to keep going. We had a deadline; we had a flight to catch. By the time all the things were out the door, or packed into our suitcases, both my mum and I were exhausted, and my son would not stop crying. The following morning, before sunrise, we got up for our flight to Uganda.

In theory, the journey home should have been easy, as a six-week-old baby mainly sleeps, eats and poops. But the reality is, babies pick the very worst situations to do all that they do. My baby's timing was immaculately off. He pooped in the security line, slept when we were running like crazy for the connecting flight through Johannesburg airport and wanted to feed when I was squeezed in my seat between two of the biggest men I had ever seen, each of them folding well over to my side of the armrest. I had no choice but to hunker down and bare my breasts. Only long after the journey was completed did I realise that for such a long flight the FCDO would have allowed me to book a separate seat for my baby, and I could have strapped a safety basinet on it. Instead, for 13 hours I held my baby tight in my arms, right over the aching scar on my belly. I wish someone had told me about the seating possibilities. I was just too tired to think straight; it did not even occur to me to ask. Advice like this does not appear in baby books, because who crosses a continent with a six-week-old? Diplomats, that is who.

Finally, we were back home in Kampala, but instead of the normality I had wished for, I felt like I was going to lose my mind. I was exhausted and sore all over, my son decided to stay awake a lot more, especially at night, when he spent much of the time crying, and I saw death everywhere. Motherhood had provided me with microscopic vision. I could see bacteria and viruses trying to get to my son, so I refused to put him down; no surface in the dirty old bungalow we lived in was clean enough for my baby. I tried to calculate how long it would take before all his vaccinations would be up to date and whether they would protect him even from a fraction of the horrors on offer.

I hunted down mosquitoes like a madwoman. Malaria was not an issue in Kampala, but I could not leave it to chance. Our house hosted an army of small black ants that got everywhere; they seemed rather partial to baby formula. What about the rats and snakes in the garden? Or the mice that lived inside the living-room sofa? What kind of diseases were they spreading? And how could I bathe my baby in something that was potentially dangerous to drink? Even tap water was suddenly scary. My husband's work required him to travel a lot, so there I was: a first-time mother, alone in the middle of Africa, freaking out.

It took several weeks, the introduction of routines and a full night of solid sleep before I could really relax and trust that my son would survive, and even thrive, in Uganda. It happened eventually. And by the time we were trying solid foods, I was in love with Uganda. There, I could pick fresh avocados and bananas from my very own garden. There, in the absence of my usual support network, I was able to hire a nanny who helped me carry my crying son around when he just would not sleep. There was our first family home.

But situations can change quickly in diplomatic life, and by then we had been told my husband's job had been cut short and we were to move to Nairobi ASAP. We had to say goodbye to our plans of quiet family life and settling gently into parenthood. We were also told I would not be granted diplomatic status or a diplomatic visa unless we were married. So, when my baby was five months old and my husband was travelling frantically, preparing to leave his post and take up the next, it was left for me to organise a shotgun wedding, pack our house and life, and move us to Kenya, all while breastfeeding through the nights. My level of tiredness reached a record high, and to be honest, I cannot remember much about our first months in Nairobi. My brain was too exhausted to process anything.

It did not help that, once in Nairobi, we had trouble finding permanent housing and had to move three times in the first 18 months. We lived in temporary accommodations and out of suitcases with minimal possessions for months, but still our son learned how to crawl, sit and walk; he was an image of a chubby, happy Buddha, sitting on the veranda, throwing the ball for our dog non-stop. We did not have many toys, but he learned to play with cardboard boxes and bubble wrap.

By the time we carried our belongings to our third Nairobi address, I was already eight months pregnant with our second baby. Although my road to motherhood had been a bit mad and rocky, my experiences had not scarred me too much in the end, so I was happy to go through it all again. Perhaps it helped that I was so tired I could not remember much and that, after a difficult pregnancy, my son turned out to be an 'easy baby'. And although I was vomiting like a proper African well-pump again, I knew I was a lot wiser this time around.

Our insurance company did not recommend giving birth in Kenya, either. Still, the facilities were much better and, since I was not willing to travel away for months and travel back later alone with a toddler and a newborn, we signed a document saying we understood the risks and had been warned. I was much more relaxed about pregnancy and birth that time around, although admittedly I did have a small moment of hesitation when I was bending over to be given an epidural in an operating room in a Nairobi hospital. I had booked a neat C-section, and we had a scheduled, swift and uncomplicated delivery. This time, my husband was there to witness the birth, and also to act as a walking emergency blood bank for me. We were back home in two days. It turned out that it was possible to plan these things after all.

The second time, I was much more confident that my new baby would make it through childhood. After all, his elder brother was thriving despite regularly licking the ball that the dog had just fetched for him from the muddy ditch. My youngest was just fine despite drinking his bath water every night, was strong and healthy despite all my initial fears.

The boys had a great paediatrician in Nairobi, too. We got to see him often because he not only cared for our children the few times they were unwell, but also took care of all the regular check-ups and vaccinations. Our second born had, and still has, a habit of developing extremely high fevers, even when he catches a common cold. I first discovered this in Kenya when he was only five-months-old. His temperature suddenly shot up to 40°C in the middle of the night. My husband was away on a work trip, so I had to summon our nanny and driver to help me. Luckily, they lived nearby and were quick to respond. The nanny stayed at home with our toddler, while the driver rushed us across the dark streets of Nairobi to the emergency room. We were all terribly worried. It took several desperate hours of holding my burning-hot, naked baby in front of an air-conditioning unit, but in the end, our doctor discovered a bacterial infection, we got the right antibiotics, and the fever was on its way down by the morning.

On every posting the domestic staff became an extension of our family. In Nairobi, our nanny took the place of the grandmothers and aunts our children only got to see on short visits. The driver taught our boys everything about gardening and how to use tools, and sat for hours with them in our car, parked on the driveway, while the boys pretended to drive it. I could see they genuinely cared for my children and my children absolutely adored them. We were so lucky to have the best 'local family' as they were always looking after us, willing to help no matter what time of day. With my husband travelling away for work frequently, I sincerely would not have made it without them.

Becoming a parent is always challenging but, I think, even more so when you are on the road and in unfamiliar surroundings as it all unfolds. Everything is new and in constant transition, and you try to make decisions based on the facts that you have available at the time. Luckily, on our postings, there were always other families around who were in the same situation, and we were able to help each other through the tough times of pregnancy, breastfeeding problems and teething pains. I was able to find antenatal classes even in the most unlikely of places, and I even managed to find a breast-feeding consultant in Kenya. There were plenty of play groups and kids of similar age. Sometimes, you might have to look hard and ask around, but often help is available.

'Don't try and do everything on your own and don't expect too much from yourself. Sit down, take it easy and eat chocolate.' This is the message I would send to the young me, the one who was about to become a mother. Otherwise, I would not change much. Stressful as some of it was at the time, I pulled through in the end, and now my mishaps, mistakes and misfortunes make wonderful memories and very eccentric stories.

Of course, I was also incredibly lucky that nothing went terribly wrong and it all worked out in the end. As much as I laugh at the events surrounding my pregnancy, and childbirth, I also often look back and thank my lucky stars.

Photograph: Margarita Mavromichalis, www.margaritamavromichalis.com

Section Two:

In-Between Posts and Afterwards

No matter where I go, my home is where I place my heart.

(shutterstock.com)

4 An Architect Builds – and Rebuilds – Her Home

M. Mohammed

No matter where I go, my home is where I place my heart.
As an architect, changing the place where you live can be an exciting prospect. However, in the case of a diplomatic family, we are not talking about moving to a new house, in a new neighbourhood, in the same city, but to an entirely different country, and then moving again every three to five years. That type of move takes away your routines and forces you to leave behind whatever roots you have grown, including friendships, jobs, and even family members you spend time with, only to adapt to a new routine, befriend new people, and learn to live in a new culture. I was not well prepared for this kind of move, much less for a life of moving around the world without having a proper settled home, so when my husband was transferred to the Ministry of Foreign Affairs, it was a real surprise for me and a challenge for the whole family.

From Place to House to Home
I lived in a city in a Middle Eastern war zone all my life, until we first moved to a diplomatic post. We married and had children there, with all my family around and supporting me. I built very good relationships with my in-laws as well. They provided me with help; taking care of my first child while I was studying at university and especially when I was preparing my graduation project, which was a stressful time for me. I was very lucky that the city was my home at the time I needed support the most.

In architectural terms, *house* and *home* mean different things. A house is simply your shelter, whereas a home is a place you have an emotional attachment with and a history. The term home can also refer to a city.

My city was truly my home, and I really miss living there. I knew every bump in our street, every turn and where each road would lead. I can still name all the families that used to live in my neighbourhood, and I can name all the other neighbourhoods in the area. The city is based on a horizontal system of side roads, for residential areas with two-storey houses and villas, and commercial streets with six-to-ten-storey buildings. In the residential areas, every house has its own garden, mainly at the front.

During the day, the side roads are bright because the low buildings allow the sunlight from both sides. The fences are not high, about one-and-a-half metres. From the street, you can see palm and orange trees in the gardens. The smell of orange blossom in March is so beautiful and relaxing. Familiar sounds, like sparrows, give you the feeling of belonging while walking in the streets, and you have the security of knowing where to go and whom you expect to meet. Locals in every area can easily detect a stranger.

All this built up in me a very strong feeling for and connection with my city neighbourhood, so I can call it home. All this familiarity and sense of security was left behind when we moved to a different place and a whole new world.

Four Organic Urban Environments

My city is of an old design, what architects and town planners would call organic, due to the streets and buildings designed as dictated by peoples' needs and the terrain itself, rather than according to some grid imposed by a designer. That means the streets are not straight; from an aeroplane, you can see how the streets meander, winding into curves, looking like snakes. This type of city is not easy to live in if you are a foreigner, because it is easy to get lost even if your house is just around the next bend, yet you can build a very strong relationship with such a city if you live in it for a very long time.

I was lucky to live in Cairo, London and other cities. They had at least some similarities to what I was used to, in that their urban layouts are all organic design, too. Most, however, could never give me the same feeling as I had walking my city's streets in my childhood and youth. In terms of my relationships with these cities, I have zero connections to them. London, however, is a special case.

Cairo is different from my home in terms of separation between residential and commercial areas. Almost all its neighbourhoods are mixed, apart from new residential-only compounds, built in the suburbs. Most of the multi-storey buildings have between nine and twenty floors. These block the sunlight from reaching most of the streets. Still, it was a very nice city and I tried to build connections with it by walking around, but sometimes I panicked when I felt unsure of where I was.

I felt unsafe, especially when I got lost even on a street near my house. This is one of the reasons I became overprotective of my children, which made them feel trapped and in need of more space. I did not give them space to play with their new friends, when they needed to strengthen new relationships. I checked on them every five minutes. If we were at the sports club, then playing out of my sight was not an option. They were the first amongst their friends and peers to have mobile phones. It was my insurance, my safety strategy, and an easy way to get to them when I needed. It took me about two years to lose my insecure feeling.

As diplomats in Egypt, we received discounts and special offers for hotels and resorts; those were exciting and rewarding given the tiring life we had. We had several holidays in areas across the Mediterranean Sea and the Red Sea. We also saw the Pyramids and other historical areas. I was just starting to enjoy the city and the country when our time there came to its end.

One city we lived in was totally different in that it is built on several mountains. So, the topography and weather conditions are completely different and unique. High mountain areas tend to be very cold and windy, whereas lower terrains are sunny and warm. It shares similarities in architecture to my home and London, the same separation of the residential areas and the commercial areas. The streets sweep around in organic, curved shapes determined by the mountainous terrain. It is sunny and hot in summer and very cold and snowy in the winter. Most of the residential areas consist of multi-storey buildings with four levels of flats (one-to-two flats per level). The commercial areas are made up of six-to-ten-level buildings that have shops on the ground floors, while the rest are offices. That separation of areas gave me a feeling of comfort somehow. Still, walking around could be tiring because the slope of the streets can be very steep. Overall, it was good exercise.

Life there was easy, with a regular, slow pace. Social life was good because I already had some family from home there and we met their friends, too. They made my life easier and gave me some support when I most needed it: during my husband's absence. For example, any maintenance of the flat was carried out by my brother-in-law, and my cousin helped with driving the kids to their school. But, from my perspective, I was only marking time. I felt I was wasting three years of my life just waiting for another move.

Being posted to London, UK, was the most exciting thing for me and my family. It was the city of our dreams. My children had studied using the British curriculum. And for any architect, it is one of the historical cities (for architecture) that must be visited. In London, buildings from many different eras coexist with modern facilities. Many buildings are centuries old. When you move around, you feel like you are walking in a big museum. Most of the big buildings were mansions in the past, which have been converted to hotels or residential flats, or even galleries. But it does not lack any of the facilities of a modern city: smart streets, environmentally-friendly buses and beautiful high-rises of modern design in some areas (mostly used as offices).

I felt that I already knew the city, even though it was only my second visit to London and my first time living there. I started my exploring right away, the day after we settled in. It felt nice to take walks, despite the unpredictable weather. The more I explored, the more I could relate London to my home. At first, I did not know why, maybe because of the many compatriots living there (some of them for almost 35 years). Or maybe it was because I already had lots of family and friends there. I thought I was the only one who felt that way, but apparently most of my family connected London to the way my home used to be during the 1970s and 1980s.

I discovered eventually that when my home city was renovated, back in the 1940s and 1960s, the master plan was based in some ways on that of London. Many of the architects and the engineers who planned and carried out the renovation work had completed their studies in London. Therefore, the influence of London was present on my people's minds before they came to the UK.

Also, I discovered some similarities between my modern city culture and Londoners' culture, which those who studied in London back then also brought home to my city. We shared the names of some things to eat and drink — like sherbet (a sugary, watered juice drink) and dishes such as shepherd's pie and trifle. Our shepherd's pie has no peas and two layers of potato, though, and our trifle uses jelly instead of jam and cake instead of lady fingers (sponge), with no cream. Since my bond with London seemed stronger and more obvious than my connection to other cities, I thought seriously about settling down there.

Relationships: Close Family, Extended Family and Friends

Cairo is a city that never sleeps; people started their day at 9 a.m. and returned home at 5 p.m., when they took a long nap to prepare for their nightlife, which usually started at 10 p.m. and ended at dawn. So, the most difficult part of our Egyptian posting, for us as a family, was the fact that there were many diplomatic events for my husband and me to attend, every day. We had events morning and night, which left our children feeling neglected and lonely. The only way we could make it up to them was during the weekends, when we would have family time, going to movies together and to a sports club with our friends. Egypt is a tourist country; there were many historical places to visit, such as the Suez Canal and the city of Alexandria. We would visit them and try to spend time with each other without distractions.

Relationships with family from farther away caused concern, too. Many members of our extended family wanted to visit, not because they wanted to see us but to take advantage of the chance to explore the city. Since being diplomats had its privileges during postings, our friends and extended family saw us as rich. They thought we should be happy to take them wherever they wanted and should even be grateful that they came to visit us during their busy schedules. Not to mention that, in our culture, we cannot reject any relatives who want to stay. The older visitors needed beds, so our children slept on the sofas or mattresses on the floor so that guests could sleep in their room. At first, the children were excited at having family visit, but after a couple of times, they were not as happy because they felt neglected again. I had to explain to them that it was rude to complain about visitors, and they were understanding and kept quiet about it.

This is a theme of diplomatic life: you should not mention how you feel to anyone. As a diplomatic spouse, you are expected to accommodate different types of people and things, to make sure everything around you goes according to plan. Then, maybe, you can have time for yourself to spend on your career, your physical and mental health and all the frustrations that must be kept to yourself.

My husband tried to give us as much support as he could during his free time, though he was usually busy with work. He knew that I found it difficult to be away from my own mother, and even though international calls were expensive, he would tell me to call her as much as I needed.

Still, the pressure did build up, and some of it came from family at home. I felt pressured to act as if it was completely normal and okay for us to keep moving from one country to the other. If a diplomatic spouse is expected to move constantly, shouldn't I be prepared for this and not complain? Family members did not understand the stress that we were under. They did not realise that diplomatic posts are not vacations and thought that we had a relaxing and luxurious life. I was shocked by the reactions of even close family members when I wanted to tell them how I was feeling.

When my husband was posted back home, the children and I stayed with his mother in another country, due to an issue with the children's education. I had to take on the role of both parents. There were times I needed support and comfort that I could not get from a call to family members. Conversations with them usually ended up with something like, 'Okay, darling, life is difficult. You must accept that. You are luckier than others – you have your husband to comfort and support you, even with him being far away.' These statements shocked me many times and made me feel even more lonely. They did not realise how tired I was and gave me no time to explain, considering me spoilt for complaining about my relaxing life. It is something most of us would not expect from our relatives, those meant to be the most comforting people we know, but, because I was living in a different city, they could not see what I was facing.

As these conversations led me to be more isolated from my extended family, they brought me closer to my husband and my children. We became a tightly knit family because we were all experiencing the same reactions from our friends and family farther away. We decided to keep our sour feelings and hurt to ourselves and only share it with each other. When you have a diplomatic life, your feelings do not matter to the people around you. Family, especially, consider you lucky – you get to travel the world – learn new languages and meet many different people.

It is true that this life provides a great opportunity to meet new people from around the globe and make friends with them. However, the constant moving makes it hard to keep those friendships. But, if a friendship is true, it will stay forever.

Living in three different countries in ten years affected our relationships with extended family and friends deeply, though the effect was different for each of us. For me, connections to the many friends I had in the past gradually weakened, not just due to the cost of calls or difficulties such as time zone differences or the lack of internet services — though these did get in the way. When we no longer interacted in person routinely, or lived in the same country, it became difficult to relate to each other's daily lives. We had been good, close friends, but we became strangers.

I lost a memorable friend from home in the sudden change in my lifestyle (travelling, having different everyday routines and different everyday problems). We used to laugh, share stories of everyday life, exchange our concerns for the future and talk out our problems with our children. But when my status changed from a regular woman to the spouse of diplomat, and I started to travel a lot and live life differently, that is when the loss began. Moving to Cairo put pressure on our friendship; it was hard to keep in touch. It did not get easier when I moved to the next country, where the calls were expensive and the internet service was not good, so we eventually lost connection.

I tried my best to keep our relationship by exchanging stories of everyday life through phone calls, but she felt that I was showing off when I mentioned a holiday we had at a resort in Egypt. She even felt like I was being annoying when I would complain about how hard it was to cope with all the events we had to attend. I had also become too posh for her when I mentioned I was looking for a babysitter because of a late-night event. Soon, I lost the excitement I once had when I would pick up the phone to talk to her. Our calls slowly changed to become just formal greetings on special occasions, such as Eid (a religious holiday).

Luckily, my daughter did not experience this when we moved to Cairo or when we moved elsewhere, because she was too young. But when we moved to London, she lost a close friend she had made in the city. For one thing, my daughter had to retake her A-levels in England and then take a foundation year before she could get into the course she wanted. At that point, she and her friend were in different years at university, not to mention having chosen two completely different courses — my daughter chose genetics while her friend chose architecture — so they could not relate to each other's subjects.

So far, neither my son nor my husband have had such an experience. It could be because of their male personalities, but it could also be because they did not develop such strong friendships in the first place. Making new friends was not easy, let alone making what you might consider a close friend. I met hundreds of people on many occasions at different events, a few of them became family friends as they had similar lives to ours, but I could not get close to anyone, even if they were compatriots.

Even when you share a similar lifestyle with someone, you can still miss the sense of familiarity you are looking for, since they did not go to the same university you did, or live in the same area. You do not share the small similarities that make it easier to have conversations and share jokes — not to mention that trust is a crucial part of developing a friendship, but my husband's job made it very unwise to trust people. His position (a Consul in Cairo; the Deputy Chief of the Consular Department in the Ministry of Foreign Affairs when he returned to my home city; Deputy Ambassador in London and so on) made people want to take advantage, so they could benefit from this connection. We had to be wary of fake friends. It was sometimes not easy to recognise these people unless a situation arose where we got to see their true colours, such as someone giving us a gift and expecting a favour in return. People whom you believed were good friends turned out to have other intentions, such as trying to cause a rift between me and my husband. It takes years to be able to trust someone, but I did not have that kind of time, with the constant moving.

Learning to be Stronger

With the absence of friends and older, wiser family members, and the lack of workable communication methods, seeking advice for everyday situations was not an option. This had a good effect on our personalities: it taught my family and me how to be strong and independent. I had to pick myself up quickly and adapt to a new environment in no time, as daily life continued right after we moved. I had to learn how to use the transport systems in each new city to be able to travel on my own, as I could not depend on someone else to help me around. Routine events give people experiences that increase their wisdom; our experiences taught us right away what others might have taken years to learn.

Even though our first two moves took us to Arab cities, the cultures still had differences and the dialects presented their challenges sometimes. Then in London, a country with a completely different culture and language, we still had to cope as soon as we arrived. One of the most common disadvantages for diplomats is that you have a very little time to research the country you are to be posted to, before being left there with no guidance.

Although the Egyptian dialect was not difficult to understand because Egyptian-made movies are very popular in all Arab countries, we still found it hard to work out how to deal with people and which words to use. My husband and I would sometimes say words in our dialect thinking they were funny, but in the Egyptians' dialect they turned out to be inappropriate — or we tried to fit in by mentioning an Egyptian phrase we had heard in a movie only to learn that it was old-fashioned. These situations were very embarrassing and made us feel even more like foreigners. It took almost the whole of our time there to learn what was appropriate to say or to wear, and how to handle Egyptian traditions and lifestyles.

Those experiences taught us to improve and helped us to adapt quickly to peoples' reactions, by turning an embarrassing statement into a joke, or handling an offensive statement by apologising smoothly with no hesitation. Through these situations, people can become either good or bad, strong or weak, sensitive or fluid. For us, there was no option but to be positive.

My children were in primary school and reception when we moved to Cairo, and after careful discussion, we decided to send them to an international school because this would allow them to study in one particular programme even if we moved. It was one of the most important decisions we made for our children's future, although neither of us had any previous experience with this programme.

My daughter had to learn English quickly to keep up with her peers. Luckily, the school was very helpful in that respect, providing her with a special two-hour daily session with a teacher who spoke both English and Arabic. My daughter made excellent progress in a short period of time and became an assembly presenter by the end of the second term. Her motivation and enthusiasm increased the more she learned; she wanted to prove herself at that school and be at the same level as her classmates.

My son, on the other hand, was still very young and found speaking slightly hard; he was very shy but enjoyed school very much. They left him to learn on his own because he was young, and they thought he would probably pick up the language naturally. He did end up doing so but it was gradual rather than natural.

Another thing my children had to face during our first post was homesickness. They would cry about missing our relatives or remembering their rooms, or how our larger family gathered for dinner, a tradition we often had back home. I looked up their symptoms and confirmed it to be homesickness, so I consulted other diplomats, who told me it was a normal thing, especially on the first post.

The best way to deal with it was to sit with the children and explain what they were feeling, give them advice on how to handle those feelings and explain how our emotions make us stronger. We also tried to give them new memories in their new country to fill that hole, to show them that each country has its adventures and places to explore.

Strong emotions give you a strong push to become a unique person, to stand out; they motivate you to succeed, to prove yourself to be worthy of higher positions in society. I was surprised and very proud of my children's efforts at understanding our place as diplomats, even at their young age. They built good personalities and characters, and became more disciplined and polite in everyday life, especially when they joined us at formal events. They became very hard-working and cheerful children and matured quickly to deal with more difficult situations.

This growing up quickly meant that my children took on more responsibility. For example, my daughter sometimes let me rest when she realised that I was too tired to take care of them and the house. She would take care of her younger brother and tell him to keep his voice down so I could sleep, and he, surprisingly, responded positively and listened to her.

Every time we moved, we faced new challenges, and as the children were growing up their personalities changed as well. At the end of our post in

Cairo, we had a new type of decision to make. My husband was going back to our home city after his post, so we had two choices: either the rest of us would go back with him, or the children and I could move to the city where my in-laws were. My home city did not have international schools, which meant that if we lived there, my children would have to go back to learning within our country's teaching programme and then change again after three years when we were posted abroad again. We decided that my children and I would move nearer my in-laws. That period was very difficult, because for the first time I was not with my husband, and I had to depend fully on myself to take care of the house and children.

Despite the hardship of being a lone parent for three years, it was a far better decision than going back home. Life near my in-laws was calm, and it was good in terms of the utilities and other services. Finding flats was easy because the city was still new and growing, and new residential places were being built every month; schools were also good, and the culture was like ours and easy to get used to.

However, my daughter, who had started her teenage years, had some difficulty settling down. Getting used to the new school and students was hard for her. During this critical time, a teen is in more need of a friend than a parent, so leaving behind her life in Cairo was hard. She also faced bullying in her new school during her first year, which led her to struggle with her grades and with the idea of belonging.

My daughter's personality was affected during this period, when her biggest support, her dad, was not there. This change made me anxious, but I was very busy trying to maintain the calm tone of our family life and taking on both parental roles. So, my daughter turned from an enthusiastic girl into a quiet and sensitive girl. I tried my best to keep her close and try to understand her, but it just did not work out as well as I hoped – that is, until she found a new friend.

On the other hand, my son was happy to be back with his cousins. At first, he was shy and uncertain about going out and playing with them, but with their encouragement and my support, he became more relaxed and enjoyed himself. That stay in that country developed his sense of confidence and independence; however, the biggest impact on his personality was the time we spent in London.

When we first moved to London, my son had just turned thirteen. I was worried he would face the same problems as my daughter, but life in London made him more comfortable with being himself. He was very excited to travel to school on his own, even though it was a distance from our flat. He made a couple of friends, but due to them living closer to the school he could not meet with them often, and they had to plan in advance if they wanted to hang out.

As he grew older, he started to show signs of his teenage years, becoming quiet and not showing his emotions. I was worried he would face the same things as my daughter, like bullying, because he would sometimes come home very upset and start crying randomly in his room. I tried to be close to him to allow him to be open about what he was feeling, but he only spoke about his problems with his sister. They had developed a close connection during the time in Cairo.

Both of my children reached the age and stages of study that do not allow moving, and since moving is a huge aspect of the diplomat's lifestyle, our children would not be able to stay with us any longer. They both knew that they might be forced to live on their own in order to continue studying or to start work. My son started mentioning moving out ahead of time. At first, we took it as a joke, but he mentioned it on several occasions, his idea being that it would be better to move on his own accord rather than suddenly be forced to find a place to live because my husband's post ended abruptly.

After his seventeenth birthday, my husband and I sat him down and explained that it was okay to feel this way, but that does not make it right to be so rash in making these decisions, and that even if he had to move and live alone, his father and I would always be there to support him.

When is an Architect Not an Architect?
Continuing a Career While Abroad
When we left for our first posting, I took with me what I thought to be the papers most necessary for me to start work there; however, I was shocked to learn about a ministry protocol that forbade 'accompanying diplomatic spouses' to work when posted to another country. After nine years of being a freelance architect, I had to leave my work. I had been doing projects on home renovations, building and such.

I became very busy with all the events in Cairo, as I mentioned before, and my children were far too young, so I could not commit to full-time education. There was no option for part-time education, either. I tried looking for volunteer work in my field, but in Egypt, to have a proper job or even to be a volunteer with no official title, you need to be a citizen, and I was not. I finally got an opportunity to work on a small project, although it was only during the last six months of our posting, with a friend who owned a private construction company, who trusted my knowledge and expertise after I gave him advice on one of his projects.

In London, as I write this, volunteer work in my field still requires some sort of title or at least viable experience. Just as before, I cannot volunteer here, and in England I can no longer call myself an architect unless I have a set of qualifications, which are even harder to acquire than the ones in Egypt. In London, I have far more time on my hands than anywhere else: my children are both grown up, and the events that took up my time before are not as common here as they were in Egypt.

I have tried filling my time with other things, such as taking online courses and reading articles, but I still feel that I have too much free time. All the friends and family I mentioned that I have in London are busy with their work, and my husband is often at work and busy with work meetings.

What is the point of wasting such a precious time just hanging around? I decided that our London posting would be a good time to concentrate on myself; otherwise, I might have fallen into depression. That would have been very easy in such a big city, where being alone, you feel lonelier. And the weather is very gloomy, which does not help.

I was lucky to meet the founder of the Diplomatic Spouse Club in London (DSCL). She explained to me the aims of the club, I really liked the idea and I joined them after that first meeting. The DSCL provides a great opportunity for me to meet people who share the same lifestyle and who have been in many of the situations I have faced. They have given me all the support I needed to get over my loneliness. I enjoy listening to them talk about their cultures and discuss all the activities possible for the club. We visit historical and architectural sites and museums. After a year of membership, I became the club secretary, which was both a great time and a fulfilling experience.

I have not travelled much during my time in England. I used to visit family or go on holidays to different countries during school breaks, which altogether meant me travelling every six months, but then I became more preoccupied with settling down in one city and on building a home, not just a house. I wanted to form a career again and have freedom over my life, so I finally decided to start a business in London, the city for entrepreneurs. This is a great chance for me, to settle down in London and have a new career to secure my pension.

Nowadays, it is not unusual to move when seeking a job, but diplomatic moves involve issues above the ordinary. Being the spouse of a diplomat, you must be prepared to change your place of residence constantly, and while this may offer some stimulation for an architect as a professional, as a person it makes life terribly difficult.

Repeated moving not only takes away your routines, and forces you to leave behind family, friends and career to adapt to a new routine, new people and a new culture -but will make you do it again, and again. You may try to build the structure of a new life, plant some roots to bind yourself to the new place, but just when you are close to seeing the results of what you have done, you have to knock that new building down to the ground and chop off the new plants growing from those roots.

Three to five years at a post is not a short period of time, but it is not enough to allow you to adapt to such big changes. And you do all of this while raising your children and dealing with their changing needs and personalities as they grow up. Moving again so soon will also have a big impact on your own career.

Regardless, there are more positive aspects to this life, as stressful and rootless as it is. My children have grown up strong and self-reliant, and I am more confident, too. I have met many people and interacted with celebrities through these connections. I may even settle permanently in the city in which I now run my business; a city I would never have come to know well without the unpredictable diplomatic life.

(Tatiana Popova/shutterstock.com)

5 Back Home: An Unexpected Hardship Post

Marzia Brofferio Celeste

The first time I came back to Italy, my home country, after eight years spent in very challenging posts, I was really disoriented. Nothing was how I remembered and expected. Changes were everywhere: fashion, buildings, streets, shops, politics, even the language had developed new words.

I felt so out of place that I worried. *Will I ever settle in happily? Will I be able to overcome my grief over friends and habits left abroad and start to feel at home again in my own country?* I did not understand why it was so difficult for me to adjust. I have been moving home, town, country since I was four-years-old, and I have always found it really exciting. So, why was it so difficult for me to settle-in this time? Within a few weeks, I found a job, hoping that this would accelerate the settling-in process (and I was so lucky to find a very interesting one), but still I felt misplaced. I did not recognise myself. I tried to talk about my difficulties with colleagues, friends and family members, but I did not find the empathy I was hoping for.

Only those who had similar expatriate experience seemed able to understand. I was surprised to see that so many of them had gone through this same uneasiness, when returning to their home country. My question then was: why? Why do I, and many people who have lived happy and successful lives abroad, have so many difficulties feeling 'at home' once back to our home countries? Even when we have chosen to return, even when we have great jobs (or our better halves have them), even when our home country is safer, cleaner, better organised, less polluted, etcetera? Why?

So, I talked to other expats from different backgrounds (spouses of people from professions such as diplomats, military personnel, bankers, engineers, teachers, professors, doctors) to better understand the difficulties I was going through. I have talked to people coming from different countries, backgrounds and levels of seniority. Their experiences of returning to their home countries are far from the positive one we all expect.

When the idea of this book came up, I immediately thought to put on paper my personal memories of coming home (I am currently dealing with my third homecoming as a spouse), hoping that some 'unhappy and lost soul' will find relief in reading this chapter, but hoping also to raise awareness of this issue among people who have never been in such a situation. Returning is very subjective in terms of the time needed to settle and stress levels, but I have noticed that sooner or later we all go through some difficulties and struggles. It is better to be prepared because there will be complications and disappointment at some point, and, unfortunately, most of us have to count on our common sense, and learning from others.

My First Rehoming

The first time I came back to Italy was at the end of 2000, after almost eight years of expatriate life in the Middle East and the Balkans. Our first post was Damascus (Syria), and it was quite an intense time. Consider, I did not know the language at all, and there were no daily direct flights to Italy, poor international telephone lines, no internet, our mail was opened by the secret services, our phone calls randomly recorded by the local authority. On top of this, there were medicine shortages, an old-fashioned bank system with no credit or debit cards, unwritten social rules of which I was completely unaware and no possibility of finding paid work. But I still remember those years as truly happy, fulfilling, challenging and exciting.

My husband and I got married during this first post; we rented our first house as a couple there; we bought our first furniture, rugs, paintings, silver. We were quite young (I had just turned 27); had no children; my husband, as a junior diplomat, had a reasonable amount of free time and we could share our passion for adventure. We had, of course, difficult moments, as everyone did, mainly dealing with health issues (amoeba and giardia were the usual parasites we had to deal with, but we also had cholera alerts, and my husband had urgent surgery twice – both ended well). There were also daily shortages of electricity: usually eight hours of blackout but at times up to twelve hours during the summer, which meant that neither refrigerator nor freezer could be used, and we had no running water. There was a dearth of cultural activities and it was also hard to find current books in languages other than Arabic, not to mention magazines or newspapers. Even decent stationery was hard to find at that time. On top of all this, a lack of knowledge about local social rules, culture and language made our daily life quite challenging. Nevertheless, in our hearts, Damascus is still the best posting we have ever had.

Our happiness and love for the country was so contagious that we had more than 250 guests in our four years in Syria. I had become a kind of private travel agency for Italians, not only hosting them at home but, also, helping organise their trips with a reliable driver (and minivan!) and trustworthy English- or French-speaking guides. Our guests were also our best connections to get recent news from our country and from Europe. The Italian newspapers at that time were only delivered to the Embassy once a week.

Our second posting was to the Balkans, to Bulgaria, and this experience was also mixed. Of course, we appreciated the positive aspects of life there very much: the countryside was amazing, with great mountains for trekking during the mild seasons and for skiing in winter; people were very generous and kind once we were able to get to know them and when we overcame the language barriers (this took us a while since, again, we did not know the language at all). There was also classical music and opera at very high level and at really affordable prices.

But there were other aspects that made our daily life quite challenging. This time it was not because of poor hygiene or electricity, or cultural differences, but due to the lack of infrastructure, a harder climate in winter, generalised poverty, high inflation, political uncertainty and a lower level of security. To make things harder, local people had a very negative feeling about Arab countries and Arab people in general, often confusing the Ottoman dictatorship their country experienced for over 400 years with the Arab culture. For us, coming straight from more than four years in our much-loved Damascus, with a very great feeling and respect for its culture and people, this was quite incomprehensible. After a few weeks, we learned that it was much better for us to keep our feelings about Syria quiet, at least at the beginning, until we had made proper friendships.

It was suggested that I even put aside a necklace with my name engraved in Arabic letters and a watch with Indian numbers (western countries use Arabic numbers, but Arabic countries use Indian numbers) in order to receive a friendlier attitude in shops, post offices, and banks.

The lower level of security in daily life, compared to the previous posting, was another worry. There were restaurants and clubs with signs at the entrance declaring 'No weapons allowed' or 'We will provide the meal for your security people: ask your armed bodyguard to wait for you outside.' Not very reassuring, right? Not to mention the number of stolen diplomatic cars: the record number was for the French Embassy in 1999 with 45 cars stolen in one year. Actually, the French Military Attaché's car, quite an old Lada, was stolen just in front of our apartment while he was attending a reception we were hosting. Parts of our twelve-year-old Volvo were stolen regularly (Volvo spare parts had to be imported from abroad and were quite expensive), so we ended up not replacing some of the stolen parts until we left the country and sold the car.

There were robberies at traffic lights in the centre of the town: if your car window was open while you were waiting for the green light, you might be 'kindly' asked to get out of the car and give up all the documents and money you had with you. Or, on the highway (only two highways crossed the country, north-south and west-east, so they were unavoidable), people would hit your car, and once you stopped to verify the damage, they attacked you and stole everything, sometimes even shoes and coats, and, in some cases, even hurting people who did not cooperate immediately.

All these security issues, of course, were linked to instability in politics and economy. The black market was very strong, and sometimes, to organise a proper dinner, you had to go from one market to the other around Sophia in order to buy enough ingredients to make a simple cake (there was a shortage of flour, sugar and eggs). Not to say how embarrassing it was to go to the market and ask for two kilos of tomatoes when many people were hardly buying vegetables one piece at a time because the price was so high and inflation so strong that prices changed from one day to another.

For all these reasons, it is not surprising that I was relieved when my husband was called back to the ministry headquarters in Rome. In my mind I thought: *What an exciting moment going back to my language, food, people, music, friends, family, culture! No more boring receptions. No more language misunderstandings. No more wasted time dealing with rules and laws I don't understand or agree with. No more struggle to get the food we like and the medicines we are used to. No more tension every time we travel around the country. Hurray, we are going home!* But (well, there is always a 'but', right?) as mentioned before, going back to your home country is not always an easy experience, and mine was not. I soon realised how difficult it is to settle in your home country again when you have been away for many years and have lived a quite intense and unusual life abroad.

This first period of planning to return home in literature is called the honeymoon. And we experienced it fully. People at home told us how eager they were to have us back: 'Finally, we will see each other more often'. 'We will do this and that together'. 'I will introduce you to these new friends I have.' It was exciting. It made me feel loved, desired and truly important. Old friends and family wanted to hear about my exciting life, about the VIPs I had met and about funny episodes. I enjoyed the opportunity to speak my native language again every day, to find my preferred fresh food in the market (not in cans or from a supermarket), listen to my preferred radio station, watch my local TV and have the pleasure of entering a bookshop and finding all the books in my language. I enjoyed the perfumes of the bakery round the corner. I had missed all of it so much and I was grateful to have it back again.

Unfortunately, this excitement did not last long. As with many other spouses I have met, this positive phase was inevitably followed by disillusionment. Sooner or later, this romantic moment gives way to a more realistic view of the world. This is what happened to me.

I started to be more and more affected by daily difficulties I had to overcome. Public transport's disorganisation angered me increasingly. Shopping was not really so pleasant as I remembered. The cafés or restaurants I dreamed of visiting again were no longer there, and the butcher, who I remembered prepared such fantastic stuffed pork, had retired and his son, who had doubled the prices, was not so welcoming.

I had to learn new rules and laws, and even the topography of the town had dramatically changed: some streets were pedestrianised, others becoming one-way only and much of the free parking was now residential only. On top of that, even interpersonal communication with people I loved and had known for years began to break down, resulting in enormous frustration and pain. One evening, I was attending a good friend's wedding and I was sharing the table with a group of university colleagues and friends. The discussion soon focused on their jobs and careers, but when I mentioned I was not working any more, and that I was fully dedicated to my husband

and his career, there was a mix of shock (I was known to be quite a good university student and a successful professional) and envy ('What a great life to be on holiday all day long.') and it was as if we had nothing in common anymore. I soon realised I had to invest more energy to gain their respect again. I left the evening with the impression I was almost a zero.

People's attitudes towards my timetable also hurt. Often I got a last minute phone call 'I am sure it will not be a problem for you to postpone our lunch to another day,' they said. "You have so much free time and you don't have many important things to do – you can easily change your programme.' Once, I was in so much grief that I came back home in tears, frustrated and hurt but also quite angry. It is easy to understand that, from that day on, I did not put any effort into keeping that kind of friendship.

Even vocabulary had changed. New slang had developed, and people made reference to books I had not read or to movies and TV series I had not watched. This 'new Italy' without doubt contributed to making me feel out of place.

I also have to admit that sometimes I, as well as many of my fellow returning expats, exaggerated. I tended to recall exciting and unique incidents all the time and I became boring. I so needed to share my feelings and experience of my time spent abroad (the good and the bad) that I forgot to listen and ask about the lifestyles of others, their changes and expectations.

A Danish diplomatic spouse, a friend of mine, helped me realise this bad habit, telling me her coming-back-home experience. She told me that a few months after her return from six years in the Middle East, her mother told her, 'We know that you have had a very intense experience, and we have loved to hear all about it on many occasions, but maybe now is time for you to turn the page and move on. Start to look at what other people have faced here during the years you were not in Europe. Try to be interested again in normal life.' It is a bit like friends coming back from a trip and inviting you to spend an evening talking about their great holiday: it is ok to listen to them for one night, but not to have to listen to their story every time you meet.

It got even worse when I tried to explain the dark side of life abroad as the spouse of a diplomat. The problem is that the general belief is that we, the diplomats' spouses, live every day of our posting abroad in a golden cage with open doors, with many servants and helpers, having a fabulous social life and a lot of money, with almost no responsibilities and a lot of fun. But nobody really understands or takes into consideration the price we have to pay: the constant moving to a new house, climates, languages, social rules, colleagues, countries, social environments and schools, etcetera. Nothing is for free. Not even for diplomats. My feeling is that too often, when I try to explain all the difficulties we have to go through as a diplomatic family, I don't find the compassion I am expecting, unfortunately even among my family and some of my close friends.

When I talk about difficulties we have faced, I am not talking about wartime or evacuations or anything dramatic, which fortunately we haven't experienced. I am referring to many small but daily personal difficulties. For example, not knowing how to get a good and trustworthy doctor; how to buy groceries when you don't understand the language; the rules about the rent of a house or the dress code for an evening with school parents; local customs regarding nonverbal communications; how to pay your utility bills or even open a bank account. I am talking about organising your move and then realising that most of your silver has been stolen, that pictures of your children's first ten years are missing and that your great-grandparents' chest of drawers does not fit anywhere in the new apartment and you have to store it in a 'safe place' (and discovering after four years that mice have ruined it and the storage company was not insured). Of course, none of these troubles are very important compared to health issues and other dramatic events, but still they happen, and have been part of my daily struggle and have marked my expat life. But one of my worst moments was when I discovered that back at home there were very few ears ready to listen to these troubles.

Soon after our first rehoming, I realised that I was not the only one. Almost one year after our return to Italy, I had a very reassuring and long conversation with a Spanish friend of mine, who went back to Madrid after three years in Syria and four years in Belgium. She described to me her experience in this way: 'My friends just don't get it, and most of the time they only see the glamorous surface of our diplomatic expat experience and forget (or worse, don't really care) about the dim side of it. All difficulties we have to face as a family, as parents, as spouses, as human beings when we are abroad are minimised, and often I have felt very, very lonely. I even have had somebody who told me, "Well, you knew all this before getting married to a diplomat, why are you complaining?"'

I also think that two postings in a row within a very small Italian community, where the culture is quite distant from ours, with a difficult and an unfamiliar language, compounded our vulnerability in these new environments. We learned to adapt and developed new 'survival skills' such as cooking without our favourite ingredients (and realising that actually they are not as fundamental as we thought); that not shaking hands when you meet somebody is not impolite, or a sign of coldness and distance, but is more hygienic for a country with a shortage of water; that wearing long sleeves and long, large trousers is not a lack of fashion, but a way to stay more comfortable in a dry, hot climate. To become stronger, we had no choice but to adapt our clothes and accessories to climate, to local habits and to availability in the shops.

Being immersed in an international environment also forced us to speak many other languages, which inevitably influenced our way of talking. We began sprinkling foreign language expressions or words into conversations; something common in our international community but sadly viewed as 'showing off', as an affectation or even boasting once back home.

My Second Rehoming Experience

After five years in Rome, we moved again: not to an exotic post, not a hardship post, not a far-away post, not a very different culture. We moved to Brussels (Belgium) and we stayed five years. I had lived and worked there just after I graduated, so I knew the town. I still had friends and settling in was easy. I also found a job that required me to travel between Belgium and France weekly, and it was really interesting. Then, we had our first child and I decided to quit my job.

Brussels had none of the exotic characteristics of our previous posts but, as you might imagine, we had far more contact with and opportunities to visit Italy. I thought that our rehoming would be easier, having kept in better contact with our country and our family and friends. But it was not like that at all.

This time, I returned not only as a married and non-working woman (in a country where a woman who freely decides to quit her job to be fully dedicated to her family is seen as from another era) but also as a mother.

I had drastically changed, and I had very little in common with most of my friends. Some were fighting for their careers, some married with little children and still working, some already divorced – they had changed, and I had changed. But what I struggled with the most was the parochialism of Italian society. It became more obvious than ever before, especially in contrast with the more global perspective I had acquired while I was away. Although I had discovered many hidden aspects of Italian culture by going overseas and had broadened my personal view of the world, I had also returned more critical of my own society.

To adapt overseas, I became more curious about others' points of view, changed many of my attitudes, and opened my mind to new ways of perceiving reality. Interestingly, once back home I soon realised that I was not able to extend this tolerance and open-mindedness to my friends and home country. It was as if I was more willing to make an effort in understanding and justifying other ways of behaving, thinking, talking, etcetera when abroad than when in my home country. I often see the difficulties I have to face abroad as part of my adapting to a new culture and country, a culture and country that I do not seek to change and that I accept as a matter of fact. And I even find this effort exciting, interesting, constructive and positive. On the other hand, when I come back to Italy, I feel actual pain when I am faced with a system and a country that is not as I think it should/could be in terms of infrastructure, people's social behaviours and mindset. It is a bit like friendship and marriage: I can easily accept a friend with a different mentality, social behaviours or priorities in life, but I cannot accept the same things from my husband. I am less tolerant of him.

The Annual Welcoming Coffee organised by the Italian Diplomatic Spouse Club in 2001 (the year of my second rehoming) gave me the opportunity to confront my uneasiness through sharing stories with other international spouses. What they showed me was that all the years spent abroad exposed to different cultures have necessarily changed us, and we have trouble in recognising colleagues, friends, family and even our town and country. We have changed in terms of life perspective, of priorities; we have changed taste and sometimes even beliefs. These changes can be very deep or not deep at all, but are definitely there, and we cannot deny or erase them.

One diplomatic spouse I met on this occasion recalled her first coming back to her home country (UK) in this way: 'The first time I went back was after a few years in Canada. Coming home was like walking upstream.' She told me she had a very difficult time, and she went through a deep depression. 'The problem is that while I was in Canada I had idealised home in my mind, and I had expected everything to remain exactly the same while I was gone. But when I got back, I had a real shock. What was very hard for me to accept was that immersing myself in a new culture had been very sudden, and I adapted very soon to a different way of life, of rhythm and even non-verbal communication; but at home I just could not adapt. I did not recognise my country anymore, and I had underestimated that, meanwhile, everyone at home had changed, too. It was like waking up from a strange dream, where everything was almost the same as I remembered, yet a few details were not right.'

People around you, your usual social network, the ones you grew up with and have known all your life, do not understand why it is so difficult for you to resettle. As described by Professor Gary Weaver, in his article *'The Process of Reentry'* (1987): 'At home, everyone expects the returnee to fit in quickly. They are much less tolerant of mistakes and have little empathy for the difficulties of reverse culture shock – such problems are not expected or accepted.'

My Third Rehoming Experience: Present Time
Six months ago, we came back after five amazing years spent in London. We all loved every single day of our posting in England. We all felt at home right after the first week there and even our two children (aged almost three and nine years at that time) never asked to go back to Rome. My husband and I knew English quite well, had visited the city a couple of times before and had wanted very badly to get a new post abroad. We soon developed a good relationship with the Italian Head of Mission and his wife. Our children adored their schools and had very good friends. They enjoyed the outdoor life (you learn that, even with rain and cold, children can survive quite well staying outdoors all the time: quite a shock for an Italian mother), they met people from many different corners of the world with different accents, personal stories, colours of skin, religions and traditions. My son experienced the freedom of moving around by public transport on his own (he was fourteen when we left), and became more responsible and autonomous. I had very good and supportive friends in the area where we were living. I was very active with the Parents Association. I joined a very nice choir and started a class in sculpture at the Chelsea College of Art

and Design. For all these reasons, I was expecting an extremely hard time resettling back to Italy. But, to my great surprise, it was not. Not at all. I am not sure about the reason why this time was different from the previous one, but I have read as much as possible about it, thought a lot about it, and I have few ideas that I want to share.

Why was Coming Back Difficult the First Two Times and Why Was it Not the Third Time?

The first element that I think has played a big role in making our/my rehoming quite hard the first and second times was that I had deeply changed: I did not change my core values and personality, but my priorities, habits and tastes had changed. Let me explain.

I met my husband while I was working far away from my hometown and we got married one year after, when he had already been posted to Syria. My parents met him only once for a weekend before we got married and most of my friends met him only a few months after our marriage. My life had completely changed very quickly: from student to successful consultant, to wife (and to 'just a housewife'). When we moved back to Italy I had a really hard time. I had never experienced the life of a non-working woman in Italy (with no children at that time), and I did not know how to deal with it. My friends were all fully dedicated to their careers, mainly going on with the lifestyle they had before my departure, and I realised sadly how little we had in common at the time: I felt out of place.

I had also forgotten the way to deal with my parents, my in-laws, siblings and other members of the family on a daily basis. For eight years, we had only weekly planned phone calls, a few letters (no internet at that time, nor mobile phones) and a visit once a year. Once back in Italy, all of them assumed we would go back to the family tradition of having weekends and/ or holidays together, having almost daily contact and sharing all small events that happened in our daily lives. I felt quite suffocated and uneasy: I had become very independent and autonomous abroad, so too many suggestions and family duties felt like real interference in my private adult life.

When we came back after our posting in Belgium, I was the mother of a six-year-old boy and we were expecting our second child: priorities had completely changed. I was again without a job and had no interest in looking for a new one, while all the people I knew had their jobs and careers to follow. Not having had my family around for five years; not having enough money to hire a nanny nor a big house to host an au pair, all my energy and time had been dedicated to my children in Rome. As a result, I had less time to invest in friendship and social life. I had to do a long school run since we lived quite far from school: I spent more or less two hours every day in the car just to do the daily drop off and pick up. I realised very soon that in Rome there are very few playgrounds, and these are not very well-equipped for play after school. I looked at the town through different eyes and noticed weakness and troubles I had never seen before. I had to find solutions to problems which I never had to face during our previous Roman experience. Except for the language, I was a stranger in my country.

The second element that I think increased our feeling of being misplaced is that, in all the years we lived abroad as expatriates, we spent few holidays in Italy. The reality was that we had decided to take the opportunity of our posting to get to know the country and the area better, so few days were left to spend in Italy. Probably going home more often would have reduced the surprise/disappointment once repatriated: a need to re-adapt would have been unavoidable, of course, but the impact would have been less dramatic. Going back for holidays, for family's or friends' important events (the arrival of a new baby, funerals, weddings, graduations,) would have kept us more integrated into Roman society. We would still have noticed changes in people, and they would have noticed changes in us, but these would have been more gradually acknowledged and would have been easier to digest by both sides.

The third element that has played a big role in the feeling of loneliness I felt on our coming back is that the harder life is in the post, the more intense and profound is the social network. I built up intense and close social connections to cope with elements such as a very difficult language; shortage of basic goods and medicines; low level of security; profound differences in culture, technology, development and extreme climatic circumstances. As a newcomer, I was helped and looked after by the expat community and, often, by the local community. I clearly remember that as soon as I arrived in Syria, I was immediately involved by the embassy in dinners and receptions (from the second day of my arrival), in order for me to meet as many young people as possible. Everybody offered me help to visit the town and discover key shops, groceries and markets. I did not need to ring people to get information. They rang me every time they were doing something they thought would be interesting for me to discover: a restaurant; the hairdresser; the laundry; the butcher (in Syria, in our residential area, there was only one butcher with a freezer, imported from Lebanon and offered him by the Italian community); the fresh market (in Sophia, there was a splendid enormous fresh food market, but nobody spoke any English or French at that time); the grocery with imported goods. Local employees spontaneously offered to accompany me around in order to translate my conversations with neighbours and shopkeepers. When we came back home, I expected a similar attitude of support from my friends and family, but nobody had a similar attitude.

On the other hand, the first factor which I think played a positive part in our settling-in on our third homecoming was that it was not the first time we had come back. We were all less surprised; we had fewer expectations and we had confidence that any material difficulties could be and would be overcome. My fourteen-year-old boy gave us a very clear answer when we had an open talk with him about his concerns about changing country again (the third experience for him). He replied: 'What should I be worried about? I will miss my friends, but I will have new friends. And you promised me I will come back to London to visit, right? This time I know the language, the apartment and the area we will live in. I will be fine.'

Somehow, returning home as an experience is a lesson learned for us. We know that there is a physiological period of adjustment. We know what is really hard to accept or to cope with (individually or as a family), and we know what we did last time to overcome our difficulties; what was useful and what was not. But more importantly, we know that we will face a more or less stressful event, and we are prepared, knowing that bad days will pass.

This is why, in my opinion, the first time we came back was the worst. Even if I had met other people talking about returning home difficulties, our experience was unique, and we had to learn our personal way to cope.

The second reason why we adapted quite so easily this time is that we had a lot of time to settle again before the movers arrived and before the beginning of school. Our apartment was partially furnished so we were able to live in it from the first day, and we decided to postpone the arrival of our belongings until the end of August, because we wanted to avoid unpacking in 40 degrees centigrade with no air conditioning. Not having to unpack or having to get organised for school, the children and I had plenty of time to discover the area: every other morning we went through all the paperwork we had to do (registering at the town hall, registering with the social health system, translating documents, opening a bank account and partially renovating our flat), and in the afternoons there was plenty of time to go to the swimming pool or to the park. On the weekend, we went visiting museums and galleries with my husband, and in the evening we went to the cinema (we had no TV or internet at home for one month) or to the restaurants we wanted to show our children. I had the time to test different groceries, supermarkets, shops, butchers, and laundries without pressure and with a flexible timetable. We were at home but still on holiday and relaxed. So, when the movers finally arrived we were ready to deal with the hard work of unpacking and organising. I think that the children also enjoyed this moving without the stress. I hope I will remember this lesson for our next assignment abroad, if we are lucky enough to have the opportunity to choose: to move into the new home (or at least into the same area if we already know where we are going to live) a few weeks before the start of the new school year, and to postpone the arrival of the movers until at least two weeks after our arrival. In this way, our energy will be completely dedicated to getting around, meeting new people and starting the settling process.

The last reason for our smooth re-homing, in my opinion, is my husband's great satisfaction in his new position in the ministry. I cannot say that it has been the same story the other times we came back. He had, like many of his colleagues, an expectation to be given a job in Rome where he would use some of the knowledge and networks he had acquired abroad. But unfortunately, that was not the case the first two times. On the contrary, he felt that there was a lack of opportunity to apply in his job all the newly gained social, technical, linguistic, and practical skills. These skills appeared to be unnecessary or irrelevant at home. His coming back home meant a return to more boring paperwork, less visibility with 'important people', fewer staff to coordinate, and less power in the office. After an intensive work experience abroad, dealing with celebrities from the political and cultural worlds, attending conferences or political congresses or debates (very often as a guest of honour), giving lectures in universities or colleges, meeting MPs or very well-known businessmen, to suddenly become a normal employee was quite destabilising.

We realised that this unpleasant feeling is more widespread than we thought. This is what a good friend told me about her experience:

'Coming back to Rome had never been a problem for me: it meant getting back to my hometown, to my family and friends. Everything had always gone as smoothly as possible, despite the unpacking and the change of school for our son. Until this year ...

'We left Paris with the prospect of a lovely Mediterranean new posting: Nicosia in Cyprus. We were very pleased and excited and therefore completely underestimated one small, teeny-weeny detail: our ministry had put a condition, a month-long stopover in Rome.

'We thought it a piece of luck: we could spend Christmas with the family and see our friends before the start of our next adventure. We filled a truck with all our furniture, sent it to a deposit in Rome and packed two suitcases for what seemed a holiday.

'My husband was officially appointed as Ambassador, all the papers – including the "agrément" – were ready and signed before the end of January and we were ready and keen to go. While waiting, my husband had a temporary job, so he would be able to leave at any moment. Except that we were going to be delayed a month or two... And then another month or two, due to problems with replacements of other ambassadors in other countries. We were told March, or Easter at the latest. Then May or June. Surely before the summer... and eventually nothing. The summer went by with a growing sense of frustration – and a very useless winter wardrobe that was all we had in our suitcases.

'Finally, a letter arrived with a date: September 25th!'

In cases like this one, not only do you have to face an unexpected stint in your home country but also a very unpleasant professional situation for your spouse, and I am happy we did not experience anything like this.

At this point, you might be wondering if coming back home after a long-term posting is a good thing at all. In my opinion the answer is yes, without a doubt. This is true even more if the expatriate life has lasted for a long period: it is probably very useful to go back and live a 'normal' life in your own country.

There is a reason many diplomatic missions insist on their employees returning home sometimes between postings. It is in order to familiarise staff again with their home country's customs. As I have tried to describe and explain, after some time spent abroad, conventions in your home country may become unfamiliar – sometimes as foreign as the culture in the host country was to begin with.

My point of view is that, at the end of the day, we have to represent our countries when we are abroad, but how can we do a good job if we do not know our country anymore? If we have not lived daily life there for a long time? And our children, how can they refer to themselves as being American, French, Italian, Chinese, Egyptian, etcetera if they have not been in the country for more than a long holiday? So, we should welcome the moment we are finally going back home! It will always be hard, but it will reinforce our ties with our own culture.

I have learned that, as with every change, the most effective way to minimise the depth and duration of 'reverse culture shock' (because this is what I have experienced) is to anticipate its occurrence in as many ways as possible. Since I have already experienced some difficulties and I have positively overcome them, I know I can count on some specific strategies to cope. Many of these coping skills can be easily taken from those developed when we were facing our overseas adventures.

Unfortunately, often we don't have the opportunity to take time to settle back in; on the contrary, most of the time we are expected to be functioning in our home society immediately upon arrival, or at least, our spouse is expected to. What I hope is that next time we move out, we will be able to organise a return via boat or train instead of aeroplane, allowing time to think through the process of re-entry.

Maintaining regular contact with friends and family overseas is a very good way to minimise the breakdown of communication during reverse culture shock. Nowadays, we have video calls for valuable face-to-face communication, especially with young children or aged parents.

The last lesson I would like to share with you is that, even though one should avoid interacting only or mainly with people who have had similar international experiences, spending time with others who can empathise and suggest ways to cope with re-entry stress is very helpful. As Prof. Weaver pointed out, 'Fellow returnees ... serve as mentors for newly returned sojourners, and can assure these returnees that their reactions are normal and only transitional.' It worked very well for me, and I have to admit, six months after returning home, it is still very reassuring.

And about the old-friendships issue, I have accepted that sometimes people at home might not recognise me anymore, just as I do not always recognise them. A new equilibrium needs to be built up, which obviously requires time and energy. I just have to be patient and remember that this process is not automatic at all, and that at a certain point the new equilibrium will be reached: some old friends will not be so close anymore, but that means there will be space for new friendships, probably more tuned to the new person I have become.

One good thing I have learnt, after my many years of nomadic life (as a child, as a student, as a professional and as a spouse), is that I have been able to select my friends better: I know many, many people, but I have only a few really good friends in different countries. And this is also thanks to new technology, which has helped in keeping relationships with people fresh and up to date. Over the years, I have realised that friendship is very much linked to the specific moment we are living. When our lifestyle and rhythm change, we will suddenly realise that our friends do not always change in the same direction. Sometimes, the friendship goes on just because it is easy, and it is part of a daily life routine. But in the case of diplomatic spouses, when we move back to our countries, we have to rebuild relationships and we might realise that some are not the ones we want, need, or desire any more. It is a great opportunity to move on.

Julia at the Bayon and one of the great heads on top of this Buddhist temple

6 Caesar's Been Hit: Life-Changing Trauma

Julia Gajewska-Pratt

After the 1991 peace accord was signed by three factions in Cambodia, my husband and I were posted to Phnom Penh. The Australian Mission was the first western mission to open after the disastrous Pol Pot regime of the 1970s, under which two million people died. The Khmer Rouge, the communist party headed by Pol Pot, were largely ousted by the Vietnamese in 1979. However, they continued to operate but were confined to an area in the north where they conducted guerrilla warfare against the State of Cambodia (SOC), who ruled the country when we arrived. This conflict continued before, during and after the democratic elections held in May 1993. This period is now known as the Third Indochina War. So, in 1991 it was still essentially a war zone with occasional fighting and a noticeable presence of Vietnamese-backed central government or SOC troops. The SOC soldiers regularly had skirmishes with the Khmer Rouge before UN peace-keeping troops arrived in 1992. Armed ex-soldiers of all factions often robbed and caused general insecurity in the main towns and in Phnom Penh itself. We expected it to be a difficult place to live, but we were young and adventurous.

We had become friends with a Khmer language teacher based in Canberra whom I will refer to by the pseudonym Serey. She had studied in Australia in the 1970s and escaped the horrors of the Pol Pot regime. Her family were not so lucky. Most of them perished during that brutal period. She had spent the 1980s helping her fellow countrymen and women who came to Australia as refugees, housing them and educating them in the ways of Australia, ameliorating their initial culture shock and helping them settle.

When we were established in a house in Phnom Penh in 1992, we invited her to visit us in her homeland, but, like most expatriate Cambodians, she had a natural fear of war re-erupting there. We assured her all was going smoothly with the peace accord, and that Phnom Penh was perfectly safe. She finally came in early 1993, after twenty-three years of exile.

I was at the Australian Centre for English (as it was originally known) in Phnom Penh at the time. I had been busy teaching and helping to set up programmes at the centre in 1992 and had had little time to travel. I decided to take a break with Serey and visit the huge city of temples, Angkor, near Siem Reap – relatively untouched by tourists then and an exciting destination that would have an impact on me that I could never have predicted.

A Deceptively Peaceful Beginning
We had a wonderful reunion. Serey knew many of the embassy staff and various non-government organisation people already, and all of us reassured her that visiting the Angkor Wat complex and many of the outlying temples would be a safe outing. She had a deep personal interest in going to the temples; her father had taken her as a young girl and she wished to revisit and remember happier days.

So Serey and I set off with her travelling companion, Daniel. We had a laugh with a couple of young Australian friends on the flight up to Siem Reap, as local planes were not known for their gentle take-offs or landings – the Russian ex-military pilots were accustomed to very steep descents and fast landings that had us 'rabbit hopping' along the runway.

We saw little evidence of UN troops except for their large UNTAC (United Nations Transitional Authority Cambodia) camp on the road to Angkor, just on the edge of town. In Siem Reap itself, the French Foreign Legion had a camp and small hospital. Other than that, Siem Reap seemed a small, peaceful, pretty town. Like most of Cambodia in those days, ramshackle huts lined dusty roads and the town itself was a fine example of decayed splendour, particularly the old French buildings, such as the Grand Hotel. Daniel and the other Australians went off to their guest house; my husband had advised Serey and me to stay at the old Grand Hotel in case he needed to contact me, as it had a radio. Technically, Cambodia was still a war zone, and the telephone system was unreliable. Serey and I settled into the old-world colonial charm of the Grand – somewhat run down after many years of war; the plumbing did not work, so we were issued with a bucket to flush the toilet! Our room, though, had a tantalising glimpse of the stone towers of Angkor in the distance.

We met up again at a local restaurant: the two of us, Daniel and our driver, who did not speak English. We had a pleasant, simple lunch, excited about getting to the temples. We had made a promise to my husband to travel by car and not before dawn or after dusk, as the Khmer Rouge, rather than SOC troops, controlled the area after dark, and our itinerary included the magical Banteay Srei, close to Khmer Rouge territory. Our driver agreed with him, so we decided that we would only drive from six in the morning to six in the evening, not earlier or later. However, having lived in Phnom Penh for sixteen months with small incidents of violence and tensions daily, we were accustomed to taking some risks. So, we did stretch the sunset rule a little during this journey.

The afternoon concluded without mishap. We negotiated our entry with the SOC troops at the guard post and then drove along the heavily forested road until the most famous of the temples, Angkor Wat, suddenly emerged on our right. The magnificent three-tiered building was surrounded by a huge, lily-clogged moat, and its grand walkway. Local children offered to be our guides for a small fee; they showed us where to rub Vishnu for luck and they climbed with me to the top of the temple mound. I really felt awed by the structure, almost to the point of tears.

I met up with the others at a carving of demons and deities churning the milk of immortality on the rear temple wall. We were treated to a lovely sunset as we wandered the gallery corridors, following strains of Khmer music that led us to some villagers, watching their children dance. We joined in with them, much to their amusement.

We reluctantly left Angkor Wat already looking forward to the next day's visit to Banteay Srei, a most exquisite temple that was, our driver said, a 'bit dangerous', as it was close to Khmer Rouge 'activity'. He would seek permission from the governor's office to take us, and he would talk to the SOC soldiers about safety. We dearly hoped to be able to go.

Next morning, we bumped over twenty kilometres of unbelievable dust listening to the famous songs of Ros Sereysothea and Sinn Sisamouth, musicians killed during the Pol Pot period, with Serey translating the lyrics. We stopped where the road became impassable to cars and walked the last 500 metres through the gentle rustlings and bird calls in the jungle. We knew our driver was not entirely happy about being here and he only allowed us an hour and a half. The SOC soldiers guarding the temple insisted we pay more money, as they rarely got any income from the main gate takings, and we felt tension begin to build in the air. As we walked down the long entrance way, a shot echoed around the dense forest. Our guide assured us it was only soldiers shooting birds for food, so we continued cautiously.

Banteay Srei, carved from reddish ochre-coloured stone, resembled a delicate red wedding cake with carving that looked like it might snap like icing. In the central sanctuary, carvings depicting the Mahabharata made up the most moving piece of art I had ever seen. The fabled birds and elephants, gods in bas-relief, naga lintels overgrown with lichen, imposing monkey-headed guards, chariots, horses and writhing characters were magnificently executed. Soon, we ran out of film and just sat, entranced by the heavy ancient atmosphere, until we had to leave.

That afternoon, we explored the ancient city of Angkor Thom and the Bayon, its state temple. Only two of the heads on the entrance walls were intact; we understood that the Khmer Rouge stole the others to sell for arms. We found exquisite carvings depicting finely detailed fish swimming about the hulls of boats, a cockfight, a woman giving birth and people nit picking, a lively crocodile chomping on the body of a soldier, men at prayer and men at war. Serey rushed from relief to relief looking for her father's favourites.

A distant booming, an eerie sound, jolted us back to the twentieth century. Serey was worried, but I said I had heard there was fighting in the south, and perhaps the sound could carry. Pockets of Khmer Rouge soldiers were active in the country, but, it could also be de-mining operations, which were ongoing. Our driver reassured us that it was roadworks. We were not entirely convinced, but we went on, up to the top of the Bayon where huge Bodhisattva heads, supposedly modelled on Jayavarman VII's face, the powerful twelfth-century Cambodian king, loomed over us, then down once more and over a pillared walkway to the Baphuan, another three-tiered temple. Again, we climbed to the top, to take photos and look down at the canopy of the jungle and the occasional ruined temple peeking through the trees — until shots echoed around the temple.

Serey dropped behind a large rock and tried to grab me down with her. I had a large white hat and am tall anyway, so I was an easy target, sitting or standing! I could see a villager with his rifle, shooting into the air, trying to scare us, I think; he certainly was not hunting. Our driver came running across the walkway, yelling and shaking his fist at the man. The children were laughing at Serey in her hidey hole and asking why she was afraid, but the incident disturbed me, and our driver wanted to go then and there. But, this was perhaps our one chance to see these sites. Serey had no idea if she would ever return. So, we stayed to walk past the tranquil pools for the king and queen, and see more incomparable carvings. We looked up to see a monk watching us. Serey paid her respects to him, kneeling in a traditional pose – anjali mudra; he told her she had three worries in life at that moment, and that she had to face the last one soon. This sounded ominous.

Our driver was getting nervous as it was approaching six pm, so we made a final stop to say a prayer at one of the Buddhas that had special meaning to Serey's father, who had perished during the Khmer Rouge period. No-one knew what would happen during the upcoming elections, so she was keen to pray to this Buddha. We returned to Siem Reap as the sun was setting, tired but exhilarated, making plans for the next day. We would go to Ta Prohm, the temple the French deliberately left for the jungle to reclaim. We planned on leaving first thing so we would catch the eerie early morning mist rising amongst the foliage and Ta Prohm's ruined walls.

The Incident
One in the morning. I felt a hand tug mine and saw flashes outside the window through the curtains. Oh, I thought, *just lightning*. Then I heard gunfire. *Oh, I thought, just a few soldiers letting off rounds after a few drinks or chicken soup.*[2] Serey, I noticed, was on the floor fully dressed.

She said, 'They're shooting.'

'Don't worry, it's just a few soldiers letting off steam,' I said, and rolled over to go back to sleep.

'But Julia, they are answering back,' she said, more urgently.

I listened. She was right; gunfire lit by tracers, the burning chemicals visible from a fired bullet, were going over the hotel in one direction and intermittent

---

2. Chicken soup was a euphemism for adding marijuana to soup and as a result some soldiers got 'trigger happy'.

shots were returned from the front of the hotel. The gunfire increased; it was very close. I grabbed my clothes from the chair and tried to stay calm.

'I am getting dressed and getting our passports,' I said, crawling, because I could hear some of the bullets hit the outside walls. One could easily come through the window. As I was trying to find the medical kit, what sounded like a bomb bigger than a grenade – I had heard grenades in Phnom Penh – landed, rattled the window and reverberated through the floor.

'Oh, s***,' I said, and thought, *Oh, my God – what if we get kidnapped? What about Serey – an expat Khmer?*

There had been a recent spate of UN soldiers kidnapped by the Khmer Rouge for publicity: what is better than soldiers but tourists? I put that to the back of my mind. It was no longer safe to stay in the room. The fighting outside intensified. Bullets hit the wall outside with sharp ricochet sounds and bombs exploded close by. I stuck my head out of our door and had a sudden, sickening feeling in my stomach, imagining Khmer Rouge soldiers coming down the corridor, red-checked scarves around their necks, hard faces and AK-47s. We crawled out of the room, afraid to stand up because of the big window at the end of the corridor, showing us tracer bullets criss-crossing the sky.

Other people, including American tourists and independent backpackers, came out of their rooms and sat in the corridor. The man across the hall, a Vietnam War veteran, said, 'I think this is serious. There are tracers everywhere.'

Most of the tourists looked bewildered and frightened, and one young Swedish backpacker suddenly broke down and began praying when the second incendiary device landed nearby. The American veteran said they were B40 rockets, the Vietnamese name for a Russian RPG-2 rocket-propelled grenade launcher. Serey sat staring, wide-eyed. Silent tears poured down her face. No one came to tell us what was going on. I thought of the radio downstairs. Could I get to it?

Suddenly, a woman rushed panting up the stairs, one of the American tour group mostly made up of middle-aged and elderly people. She shouted, 'Caesar's been hit! Caesar's been hit!' This was the tour group leader.

The American veteran said there was a doctor in the group. I went back for my medical kit in case the bandages might be of use. I crawled into the darkened room, lit only by intense firing outside, my heart pounding against my ribs. I grabbed the kit and scuttled out of there commando-style. Serey looked as petrified as I felt but I felt responsible for her and had to keep a cool head – and had to get downstairs to find out what was happening. I stepped between people's legs and started down the stairs, following the trail of blood obviously left by Caesar, and – boom! More incoming! The staircase shook. Another B40 and a few grenades shook the windows. I shuddered and kept going.

There was frenzied activity at the bottom of the stairs. Concerned people surrounded Caesar. He had staggered down the stairs and his Khmer guide, covered in blood, must have helped him. The doctor bent over him. In a lull in the fighting, a man who seemed in control of the situation introduced himself as the Food and Beverage Manager. He said they had enough bandages, and had radioed for help. The UN would come to us when the fighting subsided.

A jeep pulled up outside the hotel in a rush. The colonel who jumped out said that the SOC Government troops had pushed back the Khmer Rouge, which had taken strategic parts of Siem Reap for several hours before eventually reaching the greatest intensity at the Grand Hotel. The apparent motivation of the Khmer Rouge was to raid the Conservatory of Statues (a storage facility for works of art from Angkor Wat) and they later blew up the bridge leading to Ta Prohm temple in their wake. Caesar was moved to the jeep. I could see he had a head wound; he was conscious but dazed. I touched his hand and wished him luck. I went back upstairs with the news: the SOC had pushed the Khmer Rouge out of the town, and things would probably quieten down now.

One woman looked at me and said, 'Who are the SOC?'

I was too stunned to reply. I thought, *don't these people know they are holidaying in a recent war zone?* I was aware of the risks but was surprised that they seemed oblivious to the situation in the country.

We sat tight in the corridor for another half an hour while the shooting and shelling subsided. Later, one of the few Khmer staff members left in the hotel informed us that the Khmer Rouge had gone, and it was safe to return to our rooms. From one o'clock to four o'clock, the battle had raged in earnest.

Serey and I took no chances: we made our bed on the floor between the two single beds – after all, Caesar had been hit by a stray bullet that came through the window. We lay shivering, half-listening to the UN trucks patrolling up and down the main road and towards the Conservatory. We believed they were ferrying the wounded and possibly dead soldiers to the UN hospital.

When dawn emerged through the curtains, and after very little sleep, we went tentatively downstairs to find things back to normal. Everyone was discussing the previous night at breakfast. We met our driver as planned at six o'clock, and he was very casual about the night's events, although he said that it was the first time the Khmer Rouge had raided Siem Reap for years. He felt it was not going to be the last before the UN-sponsored elections. He was right: two more raids, much more intense than the first, would occur before the election in May 1993. The UN was keen to play down the incidents as they did not want to disrupt the election process. In 1994, a year after we left Cambodia, several people were kidnapped for ransom and a couple of tourists were killed on the road to Banteay Srei.

Our friends in the guest house were shaken, too, not so much by the shooting but more by their host's reaction. She had handed over all her money and gold to one of the Australians, and insisted she bribe her way out of Siem Reap if they closed the airport! Our driver informed us that two SOC troops had been killed and more injured. Sobered by our discussions, we decided we might as well go on with the day's sightseeing, because if the airport was closed, there was not much to be done about it. Locals were back on the streets. We were assured life was back to 'normal', our driver was ready and willing to go and so we decided to visit the temples on our last morning. This was what we did after incidents in Phnom Penh, we just got on with life. That is the nature of living in a country negotiating a transition from thirty years of war to a semblance of peace.

So, off we went. I was reluctant to go, but Serey was determined to see Ta Prohm, a favourite of her father's. The French Foreign Legion were already busy repairing the blown-up bridge. We discovered from them that the French President Francois Mitterrand was due to visit in two days, another motive for the Khmer Rouge raid, perhaps. As the bridge was under repair, the French Foreign Legion engineers advised us to go and see Preah Khan for two hours and come back. They would accompany us to Ta Prohm. We saw Preah Khan, eerie and monumental in the quiet morning, empty of tourists. This became my favourite temple, built by Jayavarman Vll in the twelfth century for his father. He also built the Bayon, the temple that possibly bears his face. According to Serey's father, it was the burial place for kings.

Then, we visited Ta Prohm, submerged in gnarled roots, vines and towering trees. It was strange and quiet to be the only people there with our one accompanying soldier. We will never experience the atmosphere again, so I was glad I overcame my fear and went with Serey and Daniel on our last day. I do not think the events of the night before had sunk in for us. We were on auto pilot and simply followed our planned itinerary. The French soldiers were not afraid. In fact, they were laughing and joking, and we took courage from their presence. We were sad to leave the temples but happy not to be spending another night in Siem Reap.

The airport was chaotic. No extra flights were organised, and some passengers on our flight feared it had been cancelled, but we were soon called to board.

As it turned out, my seat was next to Caesar, who had appeared with his head heavily bandaged, walking with assistance. He showed us the bullet that had fortunately only grazed his skull, and then embedded itself in his bedroom door frame. Caesar was suffering from what appeared to be a fear of flying but I later learned was probably an early sign of post-traumatic stress disorder (PTSD); I reassured him that the mist from the air-conditioning vents was not smoke but condensation. We got our last glimpse of Angkor through the clouds, with poor Caesar suffering anxiety through an otherwise uneventful flight back.

Colleagues in Phnom Penh treated the idea of fighting in Siem Reap with scepticism as they had heard nothing, but by that evening UN reports flooded in and news stories started to get through.

I thought then that I was finished with the events of that February night, but I was wrong.

Post-Incident Reactions 1993 – 1995

I soon began to have nightmares, developed a fear of enclosed spaces and began to have panic attacks, although at the time I thought I was having small heart attacks. I went home to Australia on leave and reacted to weapons testing near my sister's home, which was next to an army camp. I basically dived under the kitchen table shaking and blubbering after hearing the impact of the repeated cannon fire, which shook the house. I had no control over my physical reaction and could not stop shaking. Here, I was in a safe country and my brain simply could not reconcile what was happening. My brother-in-law, a medic in the army, realised I might have PTSD symptoms, and my sister's doctor referred me to a Brisbane specialist who treated post-war victims and Vietnam veterans.

The psychiatrist I went to was frankly shocked that I did not receive a debriefing, options for treatment or further support. Spouses, at that time, were largely ignored by the foreign service department, the attitude being that you chose to go on posting and you were informed of the risks.

What surprised me was that there were physical as well as mental effects of PTSD. These included intense heart palpitations; insomnia; panic attacks; shortness of breath and sweating, usually at the most inappropriate times and in situations that are seemingly non-threatening, such as in a shopping mall. If I could not see an exit, I would panic. For a person who prided herself on being in control, it was frightening to be out of control of my body and the reactions to triggers and reminders would take me by surprise. The doctor explained that the body reacts to such situations with fight or flight – mine was flight, but in Cambodia I was trapped in the hotel. There was also survivor guilt to consider since several soldiers died defending the hotel that night. I asked him why I should get this after such a short exposure to fighting; after all, my mother had endured six years of war during WWII, including many air raids and even interrogation by the Gestapo. She had every reason to suffer PTSD. Six hours or six years – it was immaterial, he said. He asked if my mother slept with the window open, even in winter. She did. I look back now and see that she, too, had suffered many symptoms of PTSD. Exposure to her behaviours may have also predisposed me to developing the condition, which is apparently common amongst children of post-war migrants and survivors of war or torture.

I had five sessions with the specialist in Brisbane, and he gave me some practical strategies to cope with the panic attacks, particularly when I felt trapped. These included using timed yoga breathing to calm the heart palpitations and checking the exits at the mall or cinema to reassure myself that there is an escape route if needed. Confined spaces, like lifts or the cinema or even high escalators for example, would be a trigger, because I could not see a way out or the end of the escalator. I did not go to the cinema for seven years, as I would sweat and shake. To avoid such places in the modern world is almost impossible. I was beginning to understand why some PTSD sufferers just lock themselves away from the world.

To a certain extent, we are prepared for such scenarios with post reports and the support of Community Liaison Officers. Still, a war zone carries all kinds of risks and not all can be foreseen.

For instance, I suffered serious medical issues due to lack of clean water in 1992. I was medically evacuated to Bangkok with amoebic dysentery, and spent ten days in hospital – and I was not the only one to fall ill. Problems stemming from this affliction eventually required that I be medically evacuated again, this time to Singapore from our next posting, Jakarta. Between this illness, which had resulted in IBS; the PTSD symptoms, and the death of my mother, I had problems settling-in at our new posting. I did get one session of counselling there, when the newly-appointed department psychologist visited the post. That was in early 1994, after I had seen the Brisbane PTSD specialist. The visiting psychologist helped, but his philosophy and advice were quite different from those of the Brisbane psychiatrist, and I relied more on what I had learned from the consultations there. It seemed like too little, too late.

It was comforting, though, to know that our department had employed a Psychological Counsellor, so that future spouses had access to assistance.

As a 'trailing spouse' you learn to accept the difficulties of going on posting: suspension of your career; coping with moving; preparing inventories; distance from friends and relatives; helping your children to adapt to new situations, cultures and languages; and exposure to dangerous situations, ill health and disease. But we also are enriched by these experiences. Living in a war zone or even on hardship postings, you become close to colleagues, support one another through times of stress and sometimes form lifelong friendships.

You can also learn about new cultures and how it is to be 'the other', and thus to appreciate what it is like for migrants and refugees coming to live in our country after experiencing the horrors of war or economic deprivation. I have now had a tiny glimpse of what the Cambodian people went through daily during the four horrible years of the Pol Pot regime. My experience led to panic attacks that lasted for years after, triggered by not only fireworks or backfiring cars but also films about war or news reports about terrorist attacks – and, of course, any violence that hit close to home, such as the time our colleague was killed by a terrorist bomb in Jakarta in 2009. Later, the spate of attacks in London in 2016 and 2017 dredged up old fears and memories, twenty-four years after the Cambodian event.

When spouses suffer because of being on posting, there should be some sort of acknowledgment of what we do and endure. In 1993, I was not able, or in a position, to complain about my circumstances, because we were expected to 'keep calm and carry on'. Also, mental illness was not something you broadcast in those days in case it affected your spouse's career.

What happened to me after the event should not happen to other spouses.

Effect on Family and our Careers
The effects of my suffering from PTSD on my family have been less significant than I expected. When I interviewed my immediate family while writing this chapter, I discovered that my perception and theirs were very different.

My husband said that the PTSD merely exacerbated already existing tendencies, such as being risk averse and being overly cautious. I was already somewhat claustrophobic, and therefore the experience of being trapped in the Grand Hotel in Siem Reap that February night merely added to a tendency to be afraid of confined spaces. Of course, the heart palpitations, nightmares and panic attacks were far more severe than my being simply nervous in a lift. This was something he understood and coped with, with grace, patience and good humour. I must add here that during the time of the incident I was alert to the dangers but not alarmed. There are a few times in the story where it might appear that we were blasé about the villager shooting, pushing out our stay in the ruins to see one last Buddha at sunset, or hearing the distant gunfire. Going to Ta Prohm after the fighting and waiting for the bridge to be repaired to go across may seem foolish. This did not mean we were foolhardy or brave, it is just a fact that living in a place, which until recent times had been a warzone, we became almost immune to dangerous daily incidents.

My husband laughs off the suggestion that I am a radically changed person since my experience, but for him there has been a positive outcome from his exposure to my PTSD: he believes it has made him a far more compassionate, empathetic and sensitive person. This revelation has both pleased and surprised me.

Without his support I would not have been able to get through this experience, but I felt my problems must have held him back. I asked him about my perception that I was a drag on his career, and again he shrugged it off. It was true my situation made work more complicated for him, but he was quite able to handle it. It was a pressure cooker atmosphere in Phnom Penh at the time and he knew he had to get me out. The UN had evacuated families, and this made me nervous and fearful. Despite his reassurance, the experience still made me feel I had adversely affected his career; other spouses have told me they have felt the same in similar situations. Imagine how it must feel to not only suffer from PTSD but to also feel responsible for negatively affecting your partner's career.

Our daughter did not know me before the incident, and therefore only knows me as the somewhat overprotective, risk-averse mother. She puts it down to my European background and being the child of refugees who survived World War II. She had also heard our stories of Cambodia and understood and saw my anxiety when we returned there for a holiday in 2009. On the positive side, it is part of what led to her interest in Asian history, politics and law. She is a far braver, more independent, smarter, savvier individual than I, and I hope my experience has contributed to her growth and not impeded it.

I never told my mother of my experience; she had a bad heart, and I did not want to worry her unduly. I did not want her to feel guilty for migrating to Australia, to safety and democracy, only to see me go forth into the arms of a war-torn country and put myself in harm's way.

Deciding on Further Postings and Suggestions for Hardship Postings
After Cambodia, we were cross-posted to Indonesia. This is when you go from one posting to another. We had two months back in Australia to

re-group, rest and recover from our experiences. In July 1993, Jakarta was still a safe place to live. The hardships we endured in Cambodia simply were not an issue in Jakarta then.

Indonesia ended up being a good place to recover. Our posting was for three years. It was quite peaceful, we had access to an excellent Australian doctor, and I found a good physiotherapist who was also a yoga teacher. I found yoga to be very calming and helpful when I was overwhelmed with feelings of anxiety resulting from the PTSD. I grew able to manage the symptoms, and I continue to use these strategies 25 years later.

I have not let the condition define me nor prevent me from accompanying my husband in his work. By the time of my second medivac experience, I had developed some resilience, and that experience helped in my recovery both physically and mentally. I knew I would get through it. After Indonesia, we went home for nearly four years, during which we had a child.

Also, today there is a very different understanding of PTSD; I think it is probably taken more seriously. And as for support, we spouses lean on each other. In 2009, during our second posting in Indonesia (2008 – 2010), we were on holiday in Bali when the Marriott Hotel bombing happened. A fellow spouse was in the Marriott when the bombing occurred, and another spouse lost her husband in this attack. The spouses banded together, supported one another, stood by our bereaved friend, and organized a wake. I found myself, with my experience of PTSD, in a position to offer support when times got tough. Also, times had changed: nobody was expected to keep a stiff upper lip.

I think my experience in Cambodia made me more resilient and allowed me to empathise with my fellow spouses who were in the 'front line' of the bombing. Bonds like these are important to develop whilst on posting. The same friend who was involved with the Bali bombing was posted to London when we were there from 2014 to 2018. This meant we were both there for several violent attacks in 2017. We kept in contact during the bridge attacks (Westminster Bridge in March and London Bridge in June). Despite living across town from each other, we kept in regular touch and she encouraged me to join the Diplomatic Spouses Club in London, where we formed some valuable friendships and supported one another.

An ordinary day – or, in my case, an ordinary holiday – turned into a nightmare. I went from being a happy, confident young woman to one who jumps at sounds and developed a fear of enclosed spaces and of heights. I have since deliberately exposed myself to these things so that I would not develop phobias. I did not want to live a fearful life and end up locking myself away from any possible danger. That would only be half a life.

By the same token, we have not become adrenaline junkies or 'ambulance chasers' and taken hardship postings specifically, but rather postings that interested us and furthered my husband's career. For example, Japan was a fabulous place to live and work. We had our fair share of earthquakes but the authorities in our district and the embassy conducted regular earthquake training sessions. Our daughter learnt how to use a fire extinguisher and, at three years of age, put out a fire-drill fire which made the local newspaper. When we experienced an earthquake measuring 6.5 on the Richter scale, we were prepared. My panic attacks did not return. I believe my experience in Cambodia helped me to cope with different situations and made me resilient and, in a way, braver. I often say to myself 'this is nothing compared to Ta Mok's attack'.[3] What Cambodia taught me was to take the good with the bad and celebrate the positive experiences we had and to face up to potentially threatening situations with a calmness that comes from experiencing a worse situation.

I can now cope and deal with the vagaries of diplomatic moves, adapting to culture shock and unexpected incidents. I am much more appreciative of what is on offer in the places we have lived. I have met amazing people and where I have not been able to work, I have volunteered, travelled and studied. I have learnt to insist upon our full entitlements whilst on posting. I am no longer afraid of asking for help and assistance. I have learnt to rely on other spouses and been a support in return. We build mini communities every time we go overseas, and it is the positive aspects of this life that keeps us going back.

Lessons Learned? Serey and Post-Traumatic Growth
Serey and I kept in touch for many years, and she came to the hospital when our daughter was born. I once broached the subject of that night with her,

---

3. The Khmer Rouge general who was responsible for the attack on Siem Reap in February 1993

but she did not want to talk about it. I hoped to see her again when we had a Phnom Penh Australian Embassy staff reunion in Canberra, but she has retired and is no longer in touch with the Cambodian Australians we know.

Neil Davis, the famous Australian war correspondent,[4] who lived his life taking risks almost daily in his work on the front line, had a great love for Cambodia and its people. What his story taught me was that we must grasp life with both hands and enjoy it now. If you have the opportunity to go on posting to a place like Cambodia, Indonesia, Japan or Sri Lanka then go for it and embrace the culture, learn and grow because you don't know how long it will last.

I recently read the book *Any Ordinary Day* by Australian journalist Leigh Sales, written after she experienced a traumatic event. She interviewed people to understand their reactions to traumatic events. Her conclusions were eye opening, particularly when she discussed post-traumatic growth. I realised I was reading about myself. I have reprioritised my life, had a child, changed my career and now work, study, write and volunteer in a field I love. I also appreciate the ordinary days and take great joy in travel.

I have had a close encounter with death, faced my mortality, shaken off the chains of PTSD, adapted and adjusted to a new way of looking at the world, but I also remember, and try to help and understand others who are recovering from trauma. My mother died in the same year I acquired PTSD symptoms, and I lost a good friend. Did I feel besieged? No, it was just an awful year, that's just life. In Australia, we live in a country protected by good health systems and stable governments; we live in generally safe, law-abiding towns and cities. When disaster strikes, we seem surprised. If there is anything I have learned from my experiences whilst on postings overseas it is to expect the unexpected and not to be afraid to reach out to others by either offering help or accepting it. I try to maintain the bonds of friendship I have made in many and varied places, stay open to new possibilities, appreciate it when life is good and never hesitate to explore the world and try new things.

I revisited Angkor Wat in 2009 with our then-14-year-old daughter, and I told her about our experience. We dined at the Grand Hotel. (We could not

---

4. His biography is *One Crowded Hour* by Tim Bowdon.

afford to stay there now they have working toilets!) Although we were not allowed to see the room I stayed in with Serey, it was important to revisit and see the hotel where we were trapped, prospering and functioning and not frozen in some kind of hell in my mind. There were indeed hordes of tourists, but I do not begrudge Cambodia the much-needed revenue they bring. The magic is essentially still there. It was as though a weight had been lifted. Yes, my mental scars were still there but they did not re-open. I appreciate those scars and believe I have grown from them. They have allowed me to embrace life.

My experiences since the traumatic night in February 1993 have been like the vines that wind around, cloak, prop up and support the ancient trees of Ta Prohm temple itself – they are mutually dependent.

Bonding time – photo-shoot with my younger sister.

1 A Child's Perspective: How it Feels to Live in a Diplomatic Family

Britten Holter

I was born in Estonia, a country commonly known for its digital advancements. Wired magazine named it the most developed digital society in the world. For instance, the world-famous platforms like Skype and TransferWise were born in Estonia. Furthermore, one of the most internationally recognised Estonian composers is Arvo Pärt and our song festivals are well-known all over the world. The Estonian landscape is flat; the highest peak is 318 metres, and the literal translation of its name, Egg Mountain, explains everything about the size of it. Yet, who needs mountains when we have thick forests, breath-taking bogs and sandy beaches? I must admit, we are a small country, with a population of roughly 1.3 million, but we are proud and strong because of it, and while we might appear to be a bit distant at first, we are friendly once you get to know us.

The capital, Tallinn, is known for its historic Old Town, which is a UNESCO World Heritage Site and is also where I spent a lot of my childhood and adolescence. It has a population of only around 400,000, so you can imagine that I was used to knowing all my neighbours or constantly seeing people I knew on the bus. I had nothing to complain about. I had good friends and a friendly neighbourhood where children could play outside without parents fearing for their safety. I enjoyed a level of independence that I learned afterwards cannot be taken for granted. I was happy with my life how it was. I did not know to want more.

My father works at the Ministry of Foreign Affairs and as such is also expected to spend time abroad as a diplomat in Estonian embassies and consulates around the world. This period of working abroad for an average of three years is referred to as a posting. Today I live independently in Aberdeen, but I have lived with my parents in New York, Stockholm and London.

Change – Good or Bad?

Travelling to another country for a holiday differs significantly from moving with the intent to live there, even if you plan to stay only for three years. I have always loved travelling itself and being able to explore new countries, although what I did not realise initially was that every move to a new posting came with a different kind of price; as they say in economics, there is no such thing as a free lunch.

Being a teenager and hearing that I needed to move again for the thousandth time – actually for the fifth, but it sure did feel like a lot more – I was not happy at all. We were moving to London, a buzzing multicultural city full of excitement, offering so many opportunities; a dream city for many. Logically, that should have been a very attractive move, but all I could think was *Not again...* I was faced with another blank slate: new country, new city, new house, new friends, new teachers and a new culture. I felt I was giving up my whole life, which I had just been able to adjust to and enjoy in Estonia. I sang in a choir, was part of a dancing team and learned cello in music school. I had everything figured out, and that feeling of stability by itself was worth staying for. Obviously, I had no say in where and when we moved, so all I could do was pack my bags and accept that we were moving – again.

Three years is an interesting length of time. I am not sure why the postings are that many years; is three a lucky number? Is this timespan somehow calculated to be good psychologically? Or did someone just pick a random number? Who knows? One thing I know for sure, this number is too small. Usually, after the first year, you feel comfortable in the country, have a relatively good understanding of the local language and have a lot of acquaintances but no one really close enough that you can count on. You have come to an understanding of the surroundings, local manners and customs, though not yet adjusted to them. During the second year, you build up a network of people and start feeling comfortable and more relaxed, maybe even thinking of the country as becoming a potential second home. You are not yet familiar with everything and there are still a lot of uncertainties, maybe even misunderstandings, but your self-confidence builds throughout the year. Finally, the third year, in my experience, is the best year: you feel completely relaxed, without any worries regarding the country itself, and have discovered its 'perks'. Knowing that you need to move again makes the time even more enjoyable, as you want to experience the city to its fullest before moving away to another place. Yet, when the time comes and you need to pack your bags and physically move, it is unfortunate and onerous to start the same process all over again – pack, move, unpack, live, struggle, be happy and then pack again. To be fair, I remember when I had just started my first grade in Estonia, and I knew that in a year's time we were going to move to a new country. I asked my father questions all the time. What country will we go to? What are the choices? We discussed all the possible options and imagined what it would be like in all of them. I was over the moon! Literally, I was counting the days when we could move and when I found out that our next posting was Sweden, I was even more excited. Our previous posting was in New York, but I was only two-years-old, so I do not have many memories of that period. All I knew was that the pictures and videos of NY were full of enjoyment, but I was too young to understand what comes along with moving to a new posting. The older I got the more I found moving burdensome. It is hard to cope with the constantly changing environment and some can handle it better than others. Therefore, I guess the life that living in a diplomatic family provides is not for everyone. However, whether all these constant changes were 'good' or 'bad' comes down to what kind of a stance you take. I am a very positive person, always having a 'can do' attitude and I think the changes have been 'good'. I am extremely grateful that I have had the privilege of experiencing everything that this lifestyle has offered me. Do not get me wrong – it has been a heck of a journey – as the saying goes, what does not kill you only makes you stronger. This lifestyle has truly made me stronger.

School Differences
At every posting, I have had the opportunity to study at private schools with excellent teachers and a great study environment. For instance, in Sweden I attended an Estonian-Swedish school. The classes were mainly taught in the Swedish language, but alongside, we had some Estonian language classes as well. I started my second grade there with no prior knowledge of Swedish. Nevertheless, I stood out with my Estonian language skills. The level of the Estonian language classes did not cater for native speakers; they mostly covered what I already knew. Therefore, I was the best student in the Estonian language classes and I even won the in-school story writing competition for three consecutive years. The winning entries were posted in the local Estonian-Swedish newspaper. It was very exciting for me, not only because of the recognition that came with it but also the small reward money, which meant a lot to me at the time. However, in other classes I struggled as I couldn't speak a single word in Swedish. Surprisingly, though

it did not bother me, maybe due to the supportive environment, where teachers were so approachable that you almost considered them to be your friends. The teacher was not someone you felt intimidated by. On the contrary, you wanted to share everything with them, while at the same time giving them the utmost respect.

I had my first experience of going to a public school when I was twelve years old and we moved from Sweden back to Estonia. It was a very shocking experience for me. When you hear stories about public schools — how pupils do not behave, are violent and are banned from school grounds — you might think, *No, this is probably exaggerated*, but through my experience I discovered it is not. I started my fifth grade in an Estonian public school. I felt appalled during the first weeks. The boys in my school acted like animals. They respected only a few of the teachers, which made them act out in most of the classes, and, on top of that, they were rude to their fellow classmates. It was normal in every class for someone to randomly walk out of the classroom or make inappropriate comments or talk with a loud voice, delaying everyone's learning. The better-behaved students, in this case mostly the girls, were not exactly friendly, either. I was amazed at how teasing others appeared so effortless to them.

The teaching methods between the two schools varied enormously. I would describe people in Estonia as rather straightforward, which often resulted in me perceiving them to be rude. I was so used to hearing people sugar-coat what they were trying to say. For instance, an Estonian teacher would say, 'You are doing this wrong', instead of a Swedish or English teacher who would say, 'Try to improve upon this for the next time. It just takes a bit of practice'. Grades at my private school in Sweden were not given on a numbered scale but instead ranged from Satisfactory to Very Good. That was however also part of the reason why I did not realise how poorly I was doing in my classes in Sweden. Furthermore, the teachers encouraged you only in positive ways, rarely sounding angry or disappointed in your work. I do not know if this is the right way to educate, but it certainly felt better as a child. I had never before felt that I was bad at a subject. There were difficulties, but I was happy to work on them. I was never intimidated to go and talk to my teachers or speak up in the classroom. I learnt how to be kind and respect fellow classmates and the teachers, while also being inquisitive and open-minded to new ideas. All of this was worth the delay in mathematics that was simply taught slower in Sweden than in Estonia.

When you first encounter the more direct method and are not prepared, it shocks you. Getting used to my Estonian public school was a bumpy ride, but it only made me stronger and provided me with an experience that made me appreciate other schools.

Another challenge I faced was being behind with my Estonian grammar and, as I hinted before, also mathematics. There were big gaps between the levels of education that I received in the different countries. In the Estonian education, the grading system ranges from one to five, with five being the highest mark and one signifying failure. At first, I was getting very low marks in mathematics solely because I had not yet covered the material in my previous school in Stockholm. The same happened in Estonian language classes, where my level was clearly below my peers. I really struggled to get back on track with all the material as well as with adapting to the new learning environment. Having so many new things thrown at you at once is extremely overwhelming, especially at such a young age. I went through a period in fifth grade where I did not want to go to school and often cried because of how hard it was. It was just after I had come back from Sweden and everything was just too different. I do not like to complain and therefore tried to keep these things to myself, but eventually I told my mother and she tried to support me as much as possible. She helped me with my mathematics homework, and my father helped me with history because he is very good at it. There was nothing, though, that my parents could really do about the bullying that was present from time to time.

I do not want to leave you with an impression that Estonian schools are bad – not at all. On the contrary, our education system is ranked very highly amongst European countries; my classmates in my Estonian school, for example, had studied more mathematics than I had. The people in Estonia are not bad, either, but I learned all of that later. It took me living in the country for a while, as well as changing schools, to realize that it is not the entire system that is flawed. After a year of living in Estonia, I changed schools and returned to where I had gone to first grade before moving to Sweden. Most of the pupils were the same so they remembered me. I got along with everyone in my class and, surprisingly, the boys were friendly and fun as well. I could see the contrast between the two schools. It hit me then, that I should not make assumptions on Estonian schools based on the last one I was in, because it does not adequately reflect what the schools and people are like.

Friends

Keeping in contact with all my friends from the countries I lived in turned out to be more complicated than first expected. When moving away to another country, the friends left behind start to grow apart from you, and the other way around. The common background that once existed, built on shared experiences and similar lifestyle, slowly starts to fade away. The history made with one group of people becomes irrelevant when moving to the next country as a new life begins for you there, so the willingness to keep in contact with those friends disappears as well. Otherwise, it would feel that you were living many lives at the same time. It just becomes too much to cope with. However, this was something I learnt to adapt to, so it was not a surprise that the new friends in the new place will be temporary friends. But, then again, once in the new place, I always forgot that I need to leave soon, and the friends should be temporary. I tried to protect myself by not getting too attached to people, but still it happened. The friendships I built up during postings did not last. I asked both of my brothers whether they are still in contact with some of their friends from any of the posting countries. Both of them said, 'no'. All three of us were really fortunate to have our best, and now lifelong, friends in Estonia. They were always there to support us when we went to live abroad. Like my older brother said, 'Without them, it would have been so much more difficult to adapt to the new countries and you would have probably ended up with no friends at all.' Despite the fact that in the private international schools it is really easy to make new friends, because everyone is extremely friendly and no one is ever left to play alone, the level of friendships was not comparable with the Estonian friends. Also, keeping in close contact with the friends from the postings was an impossible task. For example, during every posting I became very close to at least one person. In Sweden, I was extremely close to an Estonian girl living in Sweden, called Kristiin. We met at school when I just moved to Sweden and did not really get along, but during the second year we became really close friends. That was a pattern with me, at first not liking a person too much but then ending up becoming best friends. I often went over to her place where we played games and I slept over at hers. Then, the next day, we would go together to school. She was always there for me if I needed to share any gossip or talk to anyone. She also played the cello and sang in the same school choir. We were always together at school. I kept in contact with her after moving back to Estonia, but a year passed, and then another one, and by the end of the second year, we almost had no contact at all. We could not meet in person; we lived too far apart.

We did not have enough time for texting or Skyping each other in addition to our local friends. The process of leaving an extremely big part of my life, moving, and starting all over again was emotionally and mentally very hard. I knew I could never have the life I once had back, because the special bond with my friends would be gone after I moved away. Telling each other about our new experiences would have meant nothing, as our lives had moved on in completely different directions. Not long ago, I met up with my friend, having not seen her since primary school. It was very interesting to hear about all she had done. Still, what makes friendships special are the shared experiences. All we had were experiences shared years before, so she felt very distant, and it was hard to connect again on the level that we once did.

I think what made the bond with the Estonian friends as strong was the number of years we knew them; hence we were able to build a lasting friendship. After Sweden, we lived in Estonia for six years straight and that was the key period where the strong friendship bonds were formed. For example, I met my lifelong bestie in Estonia. Her name is Helena, and our birthdays are only a couple of months apart. We were only four years old when we met, but both of us still vividly remember it. It was a sunny day. I had just come back from New York and had a straightforward attitude, so when I saw her across the street, I waved and asked if she wanted to play with me. That was the beginning of our friendship. We had common hobbies. We danced together in the same dance studio. Both of us are musical people; she plays the flute and I play the cello, and we sang in the same choir. Our families became friends as well and we went on small trips in Estonia, usually camping in the middle of nowhere. I had multiple sleepovers at Helena's place. We used to create our own songs in broken English, and our own movies. We still have these, and it is hilarious to look at them. Both of us had a lot of free time and we spent most of it together. We did not have mobile phones or access to computers. I am now actually realising how much one could do instead of the time spent in front of a computer, iPad or iPhone. These really hinder one's development in certain areas, like being creative, or having good social skills. With Helena, it did not matter that I was moving around because every time we met again, it felt like we had never been apart. I have learned to value this kind of friendship as you do not often meet someone with whom you connect so well, someone you can always count on, especially when you are often apart.

When I look back, interestingly, I have never really met other diplomatic kids that were the same age as me. Whenever I went to some of the social events with my father, it was always just full of grownups and babies. In London, during my last high school year, I met a boy from Estonia. He was one year younger than me and his father also worked in the Estonian Ministry of Foreign Affairs. The boy shared a common view with me that the older you get the harder it is to leave your friends behind and thus find the motivation to move to the next posting. He was also missing his friends and found it difficult to fit in and make new friends in the new environment. It was comforting to know that someone else felt the same way as me, otherwise it often felt quite lonely. No one truly understands what you feel and, unfortunately, there was nothing anyone could do to erase the inner struggles that me or the Estonian boy had. My younger brother told me that it was strange for him to find himself suddenly changing from being part of a close-knit group of friends into being the 'new kid'. What worked in one school environment did not work in the other. For example, the jokes that the pupils found funny in the Estonian school did not work at all in London. He also felt like he lacked confidence and fluency to adequately express himself. There were times when he felt he did not fit in. Probably most people have felt this during some period of their life, but the difference was that it was because of his cultural identity, due to this lifestyle. Being the new kid means that you have no clue about who is friends with whom, what kind of history people share with each other and with the teachers, meaning that it is much harder to form strong and lasting bonds and might be why the friendships did not last.

Where is Home?

Whenever anyone asks me what country I consider to be my home, I pause and struggle to answer. What makes a place so special that we start thinking and calling it home is hard to define. I used to think that Estonia was my home, because I was born there and have spent half of my life in the country so it must be my home. Nevertheless, it is not that simple. Living three years in one country might not seem that long of a period, but every three years spent abroad lead me further away from Estonia.

Despite knowing that each posting only lasts for three years and having a mindset of the new country being just a temporary home, I still managed to get attached to all of the three places I lived. I still carry a 'piece' from each country with me every day. New York gave me my American accent. Often people ask if I am from the US or even Australia, the last one mostly because they have not heard of Estonia before and when you pronounce 'Estonia' it can sound a bit like 'Australia'. Stockholm was the start of developing my musical side. I started playing the cello and continued singing. Finally, London provided me with an education that gave me a strong basis for my future studies. All these places are special to me in their own ways, making Estonia not seem that exceptional anymore. As one can see, it is not the countries or cities that make the places memorable, but the experiences and the people.

Estonia has a lot to offer and is quite a remarkable country, however the more I spent time abroad the less I felt the connection with it that was once there. I was gradually transforming as a person and in a direction that was not in harmony with my Estonian peers or society. The difference arose because of my increasing global outlook. Living abroad introduced me to many cultures and perspectives on life, which mixed up my own. At first, every time I went back to live in Estonia it was very exciting because everyone was interested in how life abroad was. It was very exotic for people because in my friends' circle they did not travel much. I could tell them all about how I went to Disneyland; or went on a school trip to a student's home on an island, where we also had a bonfire evening and slept over; how every Saturday it was a custom to have candy, based on 'Lördagsgodis' the Scandinavian for 'Saturday Treats' or 'Saturday Candy', an idea to eat sweets only at the weekend to save the nation's teeth from cavities, brought in in the 1950s; how I went to amusement parks and so on. My friends were always extremely jealous of me and they could not understand that there would be anything hard with this kind of lifestyle. I tried also not to think about the difficult aspects of this kind of life, because it would not help. Hence, I kept the fantasy alive that I am extremely lucky to have this kind of opportunity. After a couple of months, the excitement was gone, and I could start to observe the differences between myself and other pupils. I felt that I did not fit in, which pushed me to start to change myself – the way I talked, how much information to disclose, how to act in certain situations. I was very good at adapting, but it did not mean I enjoyed the process. It was extremely frustrating. In my mind, I thought Estonia would stay the one place that would always be my home where I can come back to and be in my comfort zone. That was not entirely true.

Is there one home? When I am around my family it is always a safe environment where I know I am loved and cared for. I am free of everyday duties and chores, and I can just feel like a child again and be my true self. It is such a relief to have a break from working; having to remember to pay rent; do laundry or the dishes; deal with unforeseen circumstances, like finding that the heaters in the flat are not working or realizing that both flatmates left their keys inside the flat, they are locked out and they have nowhere to sleep (true story). These experiences teach you a lot, but also might almost feel unbearable when you are on your own. At my parents', I can abandon all my worries because I can rely on them to take care of everything. My mother has always been there for me. During postings she has never worked. She always stayed at home to take care of me and my three siblings. It did not matter if the first day at school was scary or someone from school was mean: I could always count on my mother being there when I came home to help me solve all my problems and feel good again. I did not realise all the implications of her decision then, but now I truly appreciate that my mother made the decision to stay at home rather than work as well. To sum up, my home consists of all the pieces from all of the countries I have lived in, so in a sense it is inside of me and it becomes whole when I am in the same place with my family.

Independent Life and Personal Transformation
After graduating high school in London, another chapter of my life began. I moved to Scotland to study at university, and this time not with my parents. I was a little nervous. Then again, as I had moved from one country to another already countless times, I was excited to start an independent life living by myself, not having to tell my parents constantly where I am going and what time I will be back, and finally having the chance to take full control over my life. I did not realise how much more well equipped and life experienced I was for starting my own independent life until university began. For starters, the unfamiliarity of everything at university did not come to me as a surprise, along with the change of being far away from family and friends. Every time I moved to another posting I had to leave my best friends behind. It becomes easier the more you do it, but it is still challenging. However, I found that the more you settle into the new place and do not let your emotions get a hold of you, the more you start enjoying the present you are in.

When I was younger, I was a shy and rather introverted person. I remember admiring my mother for being so good at talking to people and holding conversations. I could never have imagined myself becoming like that. Social interactions often felt forced and intimidating. I knew part of it was because I was afraid of having a differing opinion and of others judging my thoughts. Who knew that all of it was about to change? The private schools I attended taught me that my fears hindered critical thinking and being an open-minded person. We were taught to think outside the box, develop our own opinions and views and to accept that perspectives might differ. Also, those in the private schools tended to have very bubbly personalities and being constantly around them changed my personality as well. I became more extroverted. I was not afraid of what others would think of my views but started to value them instead. I began to appreciate people who had the courage to have their own stance, even if it differed significantly from others.

One of the main things I have learnt because of being a diplomatic kid is to embrace the unknown. I used to fear it, which is part of normal human behaviour. When you have been to five new schools in twelve years of education, you learn not to let your fear win. You must face it and accept it. A lot of times, I am tempted to let my fear win, but I realise that this will not do me any good, so I just do everything and see what happens. So far, it has been an effective strategy for me.

I am very proud of what I have done and accomplished. Currently, I work part-time as a support worker supporting vulnerable adults; am one of the head organisers of an employability conference at my university; do kickboxing and, if I have any time left, I take on another activity just because I still have some spare time. I have become used to a busy life and get bored if I do not have many things to do. This is the kind of person I have now transformed into. Sometimes, I feel I intentionally make my life harder, running towards the most difficult experiences and not giving myself any breathing space. I guess that is why we say that life is like a roller coaster. For me, it really has been, and I am sure it will continue to be. That is what makes life fun.

Technology keeping us close even when apart — the author in Slovenia and her daughter in the UK

8 From Ljubljana to London:
Technology Shortening Long Distances

Valentina Prevolnik Rupel & Manca Rupel

It is said that life is the pursuit of happiness. Mahatma Gandhi once said that happiness is when what you think, what you say and what you do are in harmony.

Living in a nice house in London, entertaining interesting people at the embassy and visiting numerous receptions and events is a life that people like to observe, love to talk about and long to join.

Being a diplomatic spouse, especially the wife of the Ambassador, puts you in the spotlight of events in diplomatic circles, particularly in a place like London, where almost all of the countries in the world have their representatives. Diplomatic life is colourful and buzzing with activities. But then, we are the *spouses* of diplomats. We did not choose the shiny, elegant and demanding lifestyle ourselves; we just got married, possibly to a fellow student with dreams of travelling and building a fairer and better world.

So here we are, sipping tea and discussing world affairs with ministers and royals, working the room filled with businessmen and organizing charity fairs. Is this us? Are we happy? Can we be happy in trailing around the world behind our spouses, adjusting our lives and our families' lives every four or so years? Changing locations does not mean just another travel opportunity to an exciting new country, to sightsee and to be amazed with everything different; it means *adapting* to everything different. It means finding a new house to live in; finding new schools, ideally with comparable curricula in order not to disrupt the educational workflow of our children; finding new doctors, banks, friends; leaving parents, as well as wider family behind.

It would be incorrect to describe such a lifestyle as 'good' or 'bad'. As with everything in our lives, it has bright sides, but there are many darker sides and negatives that need to be overcome and handled. There are, however, factors that make the transitions into diplomatic life, from whatever life and career one is having, much easier. One of these is technology, which is becoming a bigger and more important part of our lives.

I have been the spouse of a career diplomat for many years. We have enjoyed three postings: a short one in Tel Aviv, followed by a four-year posting in Washington DC and the current posting in London, which is also our first ambassadorial post. Two daughters fill our every day with joy. We try to continue our lives and the activities that we were engaged with at home in Slovenia, but, of course, there are new activities introduced by a new environment, new opportunities that necessarily come with one of the world's busiest cities and my husband's new working position.

All of that needs to be included in our schedules; busy days pass quickly, and there are not really many chances to stop and think about whether we feel happy or fulfilled. I am not really sure whether this is at all necessary – how often do people just live their lives, and how often do they think about whether this life is what they want? But in the end, as with everything, our current ways are a consequence of choices we made in the past.

I remember the day five years ago when we were walking in Ljubljana, and my husband told me about an opening for a London posting. 'Should we apply?' he asked. I knew what these three words meant; it was not our first posting. I loved staying in Slovenia. I felt comfortable. I was not very young anymore and stability was really becoming important to me. I got along with my co-workers and the job I was doing as a researcher at the Institute for Economic Research was familiar. It included some travelling and was diverse enough to give me the feeling of satisfaction and growth.

We had also become used to our daily routines. After coming back from Washington DC, we bought a house in a small village close to my parents. It was relaxing, as we could help each other, keeping each other company. My parents helped us with taking care of the girls, as we had to commute to Ljubljana each day and were usually quite late back from work. Both of my daughters went to primary school, they were doing well and were accepted by peers, and we all had our hobbies.

Looking back at this comfortable happiness, I sometimes think that perhaps the thought of applying for the new posting in London itself did not actually make me picture, make me realise, what was waiting for us. In the end, just applying did not necessarily mean that we would be chosen for the position. On the other hand, such complex decisions, with masses of unknown factors, could actually be processed and decided on quite quickly: in the back of my mind, I knew that delaying such opportunities and decisions is not really possible. At that point, it had been six years since our last posting, which is a long break for a career diplomat. Saying no to the opportunity could be interpreted as saying 'my husband's successful diplomatic career is not a career anymore'. So, the decision was easy, and as we are in London now it is clear just what the decision was, and which factors prevailed. The choice to follow diplomats has always been there. There were diplomatic spouses like Vita Sackville-West, a poet and a garden designer who, at the beginning of the twentieth century, decided to stay back home and follow her own career. There were spouses who could hardly await adventures and the challenges of the unknown lands, and did not hesitate to make a choice to go and leave domestic life behind.

There were also many diplomatic spouses for whom the decision to follow their partners abroad was not easy due to the lack of desire for social and public life (marriage does not magically make our characters and wishes similar to those of our spouses), the loneliness of leaving family and friends behind in their home countries, the fear of living in dangerous parts of the world and the difficulty of long travels.

In spite of that, they knew that being alongside their spouses was important for keeping the marriage and the family together, and in the end, they made a decision and left their home country. Reading about their hardships is most fascinating: travelling for months in carriages in deep snow, hiking the mountain passes in blazing sun, suffering from ill health on long journeys, losing infants and children to unknown diseases, tiredness and waiting in loneliness, not being able to communicate in foreign languages for weeks or months before finally the letters from home arrived – it all seems beyond imagination. Still, all these spouses did not give up – they made a choice to spend life as a family, tried to make the most of it and tried to find happiness.

Chatting today with my mother-in-law, who is visiting us in London, while thinking of going home in two weeks for Christmas, and listening to my daughters' friends from Spain, Brazil, Australia and South Africa speaking English with British accents a floor above me, gave me a real feeling of happiness. The changes and adaptations I needed to make worth the effort for the excellent results my husband has achieved in his career as a diplomat. It does take effort, but technology can keep us balancing career, free time and family life, if used smartly.

Travelling

The choices that we face are exactly the same as they used to be a century ago: should we stay, or should we go? Saying that, the environment in which these decisions are taken has changed completely. Travelling is easy; even if we are sent to another part of the planet the journey will not take more than a day or two.

It cannot be emphasized enough: going somewhere for years is not tourism; it is life, and in your life usually (unlike your holidays) you need and want to include friends and family. Lower prices and high frequency of air travelling has made this possible for all — travelling back and forth is feasible for us and ours, and being together for Christmas and anniversaries is something that can easily be continued. Living in London is special also due to it being a global transport hub; with its numerous airports, London is connected to all parts of the world.

Due to frequent and cheap flights, some diplomatic spouses even decide to join their husbands and at the same time keep their jobs in their home countries — their flights in and out of the United Kingdom being booked for months in advance, since they fly in for weekends or spend every second week back home, working as professionals in their own right. Although other countries may not be such travelling centres, it is pretty safe to say that the choice of moving abroad is nowadays much less influenced by the distance of the location and issues of social deprivation, but is more a decision of balancing various social roles that we wish to fulfil.

In the last few years, I have been talking with many diplomats and their spouses, and the distance, travelling time or lack of travelling options were almost never mentioned as the main difficulties. Ultimately, it must be also realised that our families and friends, not just us, are mobile and global — which makes it easy to keep in touch, stay up-to-date and to meet online.

In the Web of Social Media

Clearly, air travel is not the only development in technology that makes our decision on joining the diplomatic life easier. Various social media like Viber, WhatsApp or Skype enable us to be in contact with people we want to stay in touch with whenever we enter areas covered with Wi-Fi – and more and more areas are getting this coverage. Free of charge audio and video calls bring loved ones closer to us whenever we miss them. Many diplomats are in their forties or fifties when posted abroad, meaning their parents would have reached their sixties or above. In that stage of one's life various disabilities and health issues begin to emerge. In order to avoid worry, it is important for them, as well as for us, to maintain regular contact, as well as immediate contact when needed. As for the younger generation, taking children away from their environments used to be much harder, especially in their sensitive teenage years – nowadays online communication tools can at least make the change easier.

Talking to our loved ones keeps our home country closer and more alive. We can be updated on weather and politics, as well as discounts in local markets, break-ups and funerals. The calls are not just about being informed, they are about being engaged and continuing to feel community spirit.

Social media also plays a role in other areas, not just to stay in touch with loved ones. Instagram, Snapchat, Twitter, Facebook and web pages are useful tools for interest groups, charities and companies to promote themselves or to post their activities for their followers; this provides innumerable entry points into local society, for establishing new friendships and for personal satisfaction.

I am a keen amateur accordion player. I started playing when I was seven-years-old and have been playing ever since, with a few years of interruptions due to pregnancy and small children when I was too busy to indulge in my hobbies.

When we arrived in London, one of the first things I found on Facebook was a surprisingly high number of accordion groups and orchestras. After giving it some thought, I contacted the London Accordion Orchestra. The conductor seemed very nice and approachable, and invited me to one of the orchestra's rehearsals. I found playing with them irresistible from my first visit, so I joined, and I attended rehearsals for three years, enjoying every one of them. Besides just playing music, the enthusiasm of the orchestra's members was amazing, and we became engaged in a never-ending flow of the most extraordinary activities.

The year 2016 took us to the twelfth World Music Festival at Innsbruck in Austria. The logistics of getting all the players, percussionists and all of their instruments to Innsbruck was certainly a challenge but nothing compared to practicing the pieces that we were to perform. All the efforts paid off: we achieved second place in the advanced orchestra category, performing specially commissioned works from contemporary British composers, including Matthew Scott, Stuart Hancock and Ian Watson. For an amateur player like me, the feeling of achievement was overwhelming and almost unbelievable – of course I had to use all my social media skills again to share the news with everybody I knew. I never would have thought so, but this was only the start!

This wonderful group of people gave me a chance to take part in recording an album at Abbey Road Studios. Recording a CD in a studio is another unforgettable experience – something that I had never imagined I would take part in. Finally, in 2018 the orchestra decided to tour Slovenia. Our joint concert with SToP Slovene Percussion Project (Slovenski Tolkalni Project) in the Philharmonic Hall in Ljubljana was spectacular to be a part of and warmly received by a very enthusiastic audience. So, a few mouse clicks in England actually took me back home in the most unexpected and wonderful way possible.

Technology and social media not only presented a change for me, but for the whole family. In the new environment of London, my older daughter, who was twelve-years-old when we moved here, started to use the internet more than generally recommended by common sense. As I knew she must have missed her friends, it was difficult to limit her internet time. Discussions with her about these issues revealed that we actually shared the same view about the unsustainability of that use. Despite being on edge about the long hours my daughter spent on her devices, I felt it would be unfair to cut off the only way of communicating with her friends. So, I let the perhaps obvious overuse of IT slide and hoped it would eventually stop.

Missing friends and getting used to the new environment has a lot to do with the age and character of the person, and so whilst my older daughter was happily chatting away with her friends from Slovenia, my youngest was enjoying her new situation with her new playmates from all over the world. Less than three months after being introduced to English she was having debates in this beautiful language.

A Teenager's Perspective:
Is there a Negative Side of Technology in Diplomatic Life?
When my parents told me that we were moving to a different country for such a significant period of time, I was worried that my friendships and other ties to home would be cut off. How else could it be? I would be separated by thousands of kilometres, have a different lifestyle, different hobbies, and different friends. I felt myself attached to my home country to an extent that I could not even picture myself living somewhere else.

If you have to move as I did, your life truly will never be the same as before. For a long time, you will not be able to see your friends in school, share your homework, visit your grandparents and relatives and have a cup of cocoa with them – however, these relationships will never really be broken. Through the power of technology, not only are we able to call and text them anytime, but we are able to connect with them on a level at which we can really imagine being there with them. And what really connects us to our homes is not really the country, it is not our town, not even our house – it is the people. Therefore, if we are able to stay in contact with them, we always carry a piece of our home with us. Moving will never be easy, however, with the significant impact of technology we can refresh our friendships with every click.

On the other hand, is technology always positive for us? With the constant real-time atmosphere that technology is able to provide for us, are we giving our new reality a chance? The first year of moving will always be the hardest, since suddenly all the things that we were so used to doing and having must change. Sometimes, we feel the urge to reach back and live our lives like we did a couple of months ago when everything was still the way we liked it.

Of course, the most effective and fastest technique to do that is through social media platforms such as Snapchat, Instagram or Facebook. Seeing the way our friends and family live their lives makes us feel as if we are with them, even ignoring the fact we are in a different country. With this attachment, it is hard to accept the new changes and opportunities coming to us in our new homes, making it very challenging to make new friends and enjoy ourselves in this new environment. Technology will always have its positive side of keeping us updated, allowing us to spread our ideas and communicate with anyone. Yet, in a way, that makes us blind to the real world. Social media provides us with such satisfactory online lives we don't even attempt to make new lives for ourselves. It makes us afraid of change by preserving our old lives all too realistically.

I believe that now, with the impact of technology, one needs much longer to adapt to a new environment, build new friendship circles and embrace a new community. With our attachment to technology, we simply do not feel the need to feel accepted in the country that we moved to, as we can still feel the acceptance in our old one. Friendships are one of the most important things when you are a teenager; you feel attached to your friends at that time, more than ever. With the importance they hold in your life, the fact of breaking away from them in such a sudden way by moving will make you want to do anything in order to maintain the status quo.

Speaking from experience, you can get to a level where you are so focused on maintaining your friendships back in your own country that you completely overlook the opportunities you have in your new home. Technology does not make it any easier for you. During my first year in London, the first thing that I felt obligated to do when I came home from school was take out my laptop and video chat with my friends in my home country for hours. We did not have to talk about anything specific; we didn't even have to talk. It was the feeling that our connection was refreshing with every minute we spent online together. I did not understand how that feeling of having a safe place in friendship can be so easily transferred to where you are currently by making new friends. If anything, that feeling will be strengthened. For over a year, I struggled with finding new friends among the other students, without it even being their fault. I simply did not allow myself to feel as if I needed anything else outside daily video chats. I decided to ignore the need I felt to have friends in my new school, convincing myself that the virtual version of friendship I had was enough. Subconsciously, however, I knew this could not continue for an unlimited amount of time, as it was simply not what was best for me or my friends in my country.

Various factors helped me to reach this realisation as well as to make the difficult yet important decision to cut down the time I spent online. I remember my friends back home attending a party and it being the main source of conversation at our next video chat. They kept on discussing funny details about it that I could not relate to, no matter how hard I tried. I kept on trying to redirect the conversation to make it somehow relevant to myself. After multiple failed attempts, I shut down my computer in rage and cried in my room as all the conversations I had with my parents rushed through my mind. It struck me that my parents were right in telling me that watching a movie with a friend and watching a movie by yourself and later discussing it over the phone is not nearly the same. That was the moment I realised I was not truly happy and had to do something about it immediately. Hence, I believe that despite the barriers that technology creates for us, one will eventually limit time for communication with home as new circles emerge in our new country.

Once the breakthrough happens, technology only has a positive impact on you, as you are able to communicate with your old friends, so as to keep up the connection, whilst having good friends near where you are living, and feeling comfortable in both of your environments. With time, you will learn that home does not necessarily have to stick to one place, one country and one group of people. Home keeps expanding as long as you are open to change. Moreover, technology makes it easier for us to accept this, allowing us to prolong the bonds we cannot let go so easily.

Careers

Her Majesty the Queen receives all new ambassadors to the United Kingdom with ceremonies at which they present their credentials. It is a big moment for each diplomat as well as their spouses, as it is the first time they meet the Queen and have a chance to talk with her. The conversation we shared with her was inevitably about technology.

I work as a researcher at the Institute of Economic Research in Slovenia. Because I mostly work on European research projects with partners from

European countries, the physical location is unimportant. The virtual environment is where we discuss project development. The Internet also enables us to share our findings and to read about the advances and developments achieved by other researchers.

Being involved in research groups means having access to information that is shared across many countries, so leaving my home country did not mean leaving work. It did though, mean leaving the office as we imagine it in our first vision: a cubicle with a desk, a chair and a flower, and morning coffee debates with co-workers, whom I miss dearly. Still, these distances have not hampered my work at all, and after working from home for five years I do not feel that I missed out.

It is hard, especially in the nice, sunny summer days, to stay disciplined and finish work by deadlines, but I became used to it. As we are leaving London in a year, I am getting worried in the opposite direction: how will I ever again get used to eight working hours in an office and with the loss of the freedom of arranging my own time? Consequently, I have now started to doubt our current standards and the rationality of demands on workers to keep them closed in offices especially in professions where work is, to a large extent, individual, intellectual and without any need for physical contact.

I was lucky in my choice of profession, especially since I had no idea at the time what my life would look like. I also chose some of the additional activities I am involved in very fortuitously. More than ten years ago, I was attracted by a new way of teaching – online study. I joined the College DOBA, which is the first and only fully online college in Slovenia. I liked teaching and supporting students online. There are many worries about the lack of physical presence, and about understanding students' motivation and cravings for learning, but with the advances in cameras, with multiple possibilities for communication and meeting students, there can be no argument that online study is not an option nowadays. It can actually make study more available and high quality, as it enables experts to give their lectures online, which would otherwise not be possible.

Being able to teach students online and to keep my post as a professor means a lot to me. Technology-supported online study is wonderful and enables audio and video contact with students every minute of their research. Living in a different time zone might have been problematic, however, online study is used by students who live all over the world. I believe that the will to succeed can even beat time zones!

The further proof that physical placement really does not play a role is my new current post as a research fellow at an international organisation based in London. It is temporary, and I applied for the position purely from my curiosity and to learn more. When I was scheduled for the job interview, I apologised as I was travelling, but as I realised a couple of minutes later, my presence in London did not matter! My interviewer lived in Norway and the team leader lived in Mexico!

The world is moving fast, and it is difficult to realise how globalization is not a distant philosophical idea, but something that affects the smallest everyday things and the adventures of our lives. While my generation still thinks about it and tries to grasp it, the next generation simply lives it and includes it everywhere to make things easier for them.

And Diplomatic Spouses?
The activities organised by diplomatic spouses are numerous. We share information and contacts via emails and in various WhatsApp groups: cinema group, book club, Diplomatic Spouses Club London, EU spouses' group. The messages have immediate effect. Going for walks, to museums and workshops with other diplomatic spouses brings a spark into our relationships, and doing different things together whenever the time allows makes official meetings more pleasant, vibrant and fun.

The world is fast moving – just as people will probably never be able to solve the mystery of what came first, the chicken or the egg, it is probably also difficult to say whether the faster world and our needs made social media popular or whether it was social media that made the world more connected and swifter. As long as we are careful to make the use of new technology sustainable and use it wisely, its overwhelmingly positive effects will make diplomatic life easier.

Photograph: Margarita Mavromichalis, www.margaritamavromichalis.com

Section Three:
Lifelong Reflections

Ilona Kenkadze

9 Adjusting: a Professional, a Mum and a Diplomat's Wife

Ilona Kenkadze

It is said that an international transfer is a major life event consisting of a mix of excitement and stress, joy and exhaustion, which has a typical pattern of ups and downs that affects the life of a family. This adjustment cycle starts when you leave home and ends with your eventual relocation back home, including preparation, culture shock, new-area adaptation and welcome-back-home adaptation.

Some families do not experience each of these stages – people are different – but I must admit we were affected by all of them. We had mixed emotions: we were excited about the beginning of our new life in a new location and, at the same time, had to deal with our emotional reactions to leaving friends and family back in Tbilisi, in Georgia.

Each family member had their own feelings about the move, and we had regular family discussions about everything related to the new posting. Sometimes, we did not even want to relocate at all. However, information is power, and it helps reduce anxiety, so I started looking for available resources in books and on the Internet, studying other people's experience. It helped.

When we arrived in the UK, we felt very lucky, because everybody was welcoming and pleasant, friendly and hospitable, which made it easier to get to know our new life and all the things that worked differently. Then, a period of missing our old life at home started. We missed everything: friends, relatives, food, even wandering the streets in Tbilisi. Time passed, and cultural differences that made us feel excited at the beginning of our journey started to get boring as everything that had been unfamiliar became part of our daily lives. Sometimes we felt stressed and unhappy.

But this period also passed, as everything is temporary in our world. We learned to cope with all the challenges and felt less frustrated. We started to live a full life. And then – the time to go back home arrived.

I will share my personal experience of how I managed to adapt to life in the UK and to life back in Georgia, focussing on three indispensable parts of my life.

The Story of a Professional
For a professional, the pros and cons of being a diplomat's wife are so sophisticatedly interconnected that you may begin by describing a positive aspect and find that you have smoothly moved into describing a negative aspect, and vice versa.

Since I am a specialist in the English language and literature, I was lucky my husband was posted to Great Britain twice; to go there was a daydream of every student at my institute's English faculty. At the beginning of the eighties, however, at the height of the Cold War, there were few chances to get to the 'stronghold of capitalism' (the Soviet derogatory cliché of London), or it could be said there was no chance at all. Nevertheless, I did my best, mastering English while a student so that I earned multiple degrees from the Tbilisi Ilia Chavchavadze State Institute of Foreign Languages and started teaching English. Imagine how excited I felt when my husband told me that he had been appointed to a position at the Georgian Embassy to the UK. My dream had come true – I had been given an opportunity to apply and to deepen my knowledge, and I believed my English skills would turn out to be crucial for the survival of our family in the new environment.

I started thinking about my life in London well ahead of time, imagining every day I would spend in the city I had always longed to visit. The first thing I did was to free some space in the corner of my room and start to put there every little thing I thought would be necessary in my new life in London. Ironically, when the time to pack our suitcases came and I sorted out my corner, I realized that many items were put there just because I was too thrilled in the beginning. This was mostly kitchen stuff like spoons, forks, knives in a set of twelve pieces, which could be easily bought upon arrival in London, or bedlinen which I was told would be the wrong size for the beds we would have at the London property.

Being used to the active life of a working mum back home, I did not want to lose my chance of working in the UK. Furthermore, the salary of a Georgian diplomat in the UK is so small, and at the same time, as is widely acknowledged, life in London is so expensive, that I realized I needed to do something. With two kids still in education, my husband and I both needed to support our family financially.

I found courage in myself to start searching for a job. But nothing comes easy; here we reach the negative side of things that I mentioned earlier. Having completed my degrees – a PhD in English philology and master's degree in teaching English – in Georgia, I was not able to find a teaching job in London as it takes special UK qualifications to be allowed to teach there. To apply, to study and to get a certificate in teaching would not be an easy job and would cost too much time, energy and money. So, having absorbed the idea that I would not get a teaching role in London, I looked for any job at which I could succeed. First, I found online a few agencies that specialized in assisting those searching for administrative roles in the capital. It took a few interviews to get an offer for something I liked. Having been in contact with my 'colleagues' – other spouses of diplomats, from different countries – I found out that they had the same challenges. Most of us had had to say goodbye to our professional lives.

I must say that the long road to my first job in London was full of stress. I was going to job interviews, for positions in administrative and teaching areas, but all my efforts ended with no result. And the most unbearable time was coming back home and waiting for the offer after the interviews. At one point, I even wanted to give up. However, my husband supported me, standing by my side and encouraging me to go on with the search. *Fortuna fortes adjuvant* says the ancient Roman wisdom – fortune favours the bold – and I was lucky to get a job in global mobility within the Human Resources Department Head Office of a prestigious British company. A whole different world opened up for me when I had to live up to the expectations of my employers. While people at work were all friendly and hospitable, there was no 'red carpet' anymore. I mean, I was just an ordinary employee without any of the special attention or treatment that I used to have at home. Everybody expected you to settle in and get on with work and life. This was one of the hardest parts of the adjustment cycle, along with stress and homesickness. Everything was new. First of all, I had to commute for an hour and a half every day to and from work. At home, it was just a fifteen-minute walk to get to the University. Secondly, as I have never worked in the field of Human Resources before, it was like exploring Mars for me. In addition, an open-plan office with around seventy people sitting in one space made me feel quite uncomfortable. I fully understood this was part of the deal, but it was very hard to go though.

The job I was doing was new for me, but luckily my mathematical and linguistic skills helped me to grasp even the most sophisticated of human resources responsibilities within the first months. However, I have to say that I felt no less stressed while exploring the uncharted waters of HR International Mobility than Columbus in his search for the Indies. In the first month of that job, I would get so tired that I could not move my fingers or toes. I still recall my husband's surprised face when he looked at me, immobile and numb, as he drove me home, before I got used to the long morning and evening commute.

What made me less depressed was that I could see I was not alone. People were running to and fro during rush hour and people with common experiences helped me a lot. Step by step, I found myself better equipped to deal with everything around me.

I turned my not-so-pleasant journey of nightmare rushing from one platform to another to catch the trains I needed into a positive experience. Not to waste three hours of my day, I started reading free newspapers on the Tube, writing out and memorizing English phrases, including the slang so richly reflected in the tabloid.

Thus, I rediscovered London in linguistic terms. Back at home we were taught სამეფო ინგლისური - Royal English, so everyone who has ever lived in London can understand how stressed I got when I heard people speaking an English that was quite far away from the Queen's English. It took me some time before I could understand some of my colleagues at work and people in the street, especially those who were from Northern England or elsewhere in the world.

Within three years of beginning my linguistic endeavour, I could grasp the gist of spoken English. My linguistic mission in the UK was successfully accomplished. My husband's three-year rotation expired, and I accompanied him back home to Tbilisi, where I continued my teaching activity with more confidence. Once again, positive and negative aspects of my professional life as a diplomatic wife were interrelated.

When we were notified of the date of our relocation back to Georgia, our family used all the experience we gained during our relocation to the UK to make the move home as smooth as possible. We understood that not only had our home country changed during our time abroad, but we ourselves had changed. Our will to go back home was so strong that we were willing to meet those challenges.

Of course, the cycle of adjustment did not stop there.

Heraclitus once observed that you cannot step into the same river twice. But when, after four years of working in Georgia, my husband was seconded to the Embassy of Georgia to the United Kingdom for the second time, I started doubting the great Greek's philosophical claim.

Honestly speaking, in the beginning, I was not at all in the mood to accompany my husband to the UK again. I doubted whether I wanted to leave everything behind me and start my professional life from scratch in London once more. I had the most interesting job working with hundreds of students who embellished my professional life in Tbilisi. To drop all that and come to Britain was not an easy decision to make, but I had to make that professional sacrifice again for one main reason: to be with my family.

When I arrived, though, I realized that Heraclitus was right. I plunged into the same river but into totally different waters. In professional terms, my second experience happened to be far more challenging than the previous one. The requirement to have a special certificate to teach in the UK was still in force, so I had to put up with the idea that for four more years of my husband's posting I would be deprived of the pleasure of doing my favourite job – teaching.

Although this second posting was to the same country as the first one, all our old friends had left the UK for home or to new postings. All our family members had to start from scratch: a new school class for our son, new work colleagues for my husband, new friends and environment for me.

From the very first day we arrived, I started applying for vacancies, but it took me almost a year before I was hired by one of the London-based relocation companies. You can only imagine how difficult and stressful my life was during this year of job searching. I must admit that I had huge help from the Diplomatic Spouses Club of London (DSCL), which I had the honour to join. I am very grateful to DSCL, as its activities and its members' support, headed by its president, helped me not to feel abandoned, alone and useless during my job search.

And, again, three years of routine – happy to have a job but doing something I did not like. I was lucky to find work and at the same time was exhausted every day. I did my job meticulously, but never forgot my main passion – teaching and mastering English. So, I continued working on the subject of my PhD research – Psycholinguistic and Pragmatical Parameters of Perception and Decoding of Irony – and took part in the annual International Academic Forum (IAFOR) conferences, which were organised in Brighton. This was really one of the relaxing, motivating and inspiring experiences for me – I was happy to go back to my favourite activities, related to teaching. I attended the conferences three times. I learnt a lot of new approaches and methods of teaching English from people from countries all over the world. I met professionals with interesting views on teaching English and spent some free time in the evenings on Brighton Pier, enjoying every moment with my sister, who joined me for a weekend during my first conference, and my husband, who joined me for the second time. To summarize: although I was not able to work as a teacher or lecturer in London, I was able to explore myself through a second profession in global mobility, which gave me more confidence. Despite the rigours of finding and performing a job, I worked on improving my English and on expanding my doctoral project. After adjusting back to Tbilisi and becoming a teacher again, it was still difficult to go around the same cycle of adjustment when my husband was posted to London the second time, still difficult to find a job and to start all over again.

The Story of a Mum

The most difficult part of being a diplomat's wife for me is being a mum, particularly as a Georgian mother who is often called 'Crazy Mum'. As my husband explains, this term is a mum who looks after, protects and babysits her child with an overdose of care. There is a certain truth in such categorization, when you think of all the sacrifices a Georgian mum makes for her child. I understand that all mums love their children, but a Georgian mother will make any kind of compromise when it comes to her job, her professional career or even her health and life, because she never puts anything ahead of her child's well-being and educational prospects.

Many of us have realized the influence on kids of living in a culture foreign to them, and experts have developed the term Third Culture Kid, or TCK, to refer to children and teens who have spent parts of their childhood living with different cultural influences. There has been much debate on the pros (ease of social skills, acceptance of multiple views and beliefs, increased language aptitude) and cons (detachment from relationships, stifled identity, lack of belonging) of what a TCK can experience in another culture. I believe that TCK phenomena took a better rather than worse part in my sons' lives, as they developed an excellent habit to get along with all kinds of people in various situations – with young or old at school/university, or in the street.

When our family first came to London, my elder son started his university course, while my younger son was still at school. We were all overwhelmed with emotions, thoughts and fears. I worried about everything involving my sons, especially about how they would adjust to new cultural, linguistic and educational reality. With proper awareness and attention from me, when I was especially concerned about bullying at school, I thought their experience of the move could change from something potentially harmful to a beneficial life event.

In addition, back at home they both had the highest marks in all subjects, but the major foreign language taught was German. Of course, they additionally studied English, but I wondered whether their proficiency in English would be sufficient for success at a British school and university.

To my relief, our elder son, having finished a one-year course with Merit at Holborn College, successfully completed his course in Law and graduated from the University of Westminster. He had to work hard to achieve this, as he had to stay in London at the university dormitory for the last year of his studies, with all the consequences of taking care of himself after our family left the UK due to my husband's post back in Tbilisi. My elder son continued to learn, continued to grow, and, by the time he returned home, was proficient in English, had become a real professional in the field of Contractual Law and an expert at living in the host country. I, as a mum, was happy for him and proud of him, especially when he was a success in starting a job at the Ministry of Justice of Georgia after returning home.

For my younger son, things went a little bit differently. He studied at one of the state schools in south-west London. We were lucky and did not have to wait for long to be allocated a place, although this is something a family needs to think about ahead of relocation. So, as soon as my husband arrived in the UK, he applied to three state schools. By the time the plane carrying the rest of us landed in London three months later, we already knew which school our son was going to attend.

Within a few weeks, his English became fluent. He was a great success in English, maths and all other subjects, and was even chosen to represent the school at a public speaking competition where his team won third place among all London schools (state, grammar, and private). I was the happiest mother on the planet.

Three successful years passed, and we had started preparing to go back home to Georgia when, all of a sudden, just a couple of months before our departure, the school nominated my son (based on his outstanding academic record) as the best student to continue his studies at Oundle School, one of the prestigious £30,000-a-year boarding schools in the UK. Of course, I understood this was a recognition of my son's achievements in a long educational journey, and of course, it was a once-in-a-lifetime opportunity for him. All the family appreciated that the school had chosen him. I surfed the net and learned that almost all who left this boarding school continued their studies either at Cambridge or at Oxford. I was absolutely sure my son would be the best student at boarding school, too, and would end up at one of these two world-famous universities, but...

There is always that little but which, in our family's case, was staggering rather than little. Without exaggeration, this presented the biggest dilemma of my family life: on one hand, I fully realized the merits of our son's studying at this boarding school; on the other hand, I could not imagine going back home and leaving my fourteen-year-old son alone in the UK. I felt appalled.

Firstly, a Georgian citizen needs a visa to enter the UK, and it takes some time to obtain one; in an emergency I would not be able to be with my son the same day but would have to wait for the visa. Secondly, I would lose my son culturally. By the time he finished his studies, my son might have become a typical British young man, who would have lost any touch with his Georgian homeland: its language, culture and way of life. Even summer holidays spent in Georgia would not help, I thought.

The worst thing about this situation was that, although the whole family was involved in every-day discussions of what to do, I was the one who had to take the decision, whether to send our son to the boarding school or take him back home with us. My husband diplomatically distanced himself from the decision-making process. It took me about two months – the two most anxious months of my life – to arrive at a conclusion: we all needed my son back home with us.

I must admit that when we arrived in Tbilisi my son adapted quite quickly to the new 'old' environment, and within a few weeks he again succeeded in his studies. Time has passed, and I can say that I made the right decision.

The Story of a Wife

Adjusting your life to the life of your spouse-diplomat is equally hard, I believe, regardless of whether you are male or female. I have heard many stories of families falling apart when they are reunited, as their experiences have made them strangers to each other, which led to a divorce, because the non-diplomatic spouse did not wish to follow the diplomatic spouse to the specific country of posting. I was lucky and have been satisfied so far with the country where my husband was assigned to serve. The UK is a country where, perhaps, everybody in Georgia would choose to live without much hesitation.

However, I have often had to think about what my reaction would be if my husband were assigned to serve in a country where stability and safety is not guaranteed at all. There were times when my husband participated in missions where I was advised not to accompany him. First, it was the OSCE (Organization for Security and Co-operation in Europe, which deals with arms control, border management, and conflict prevention and resolution) in Albania and then the UNAMET mission (United Nations Mission in East Timor). I was strongly advised not to follow my husband, since these locations were indeed quite dangerous at the time. During those two missions of six months each, I had to support our family and kids back in Georgia by myself. That was in the nineteen nineties, when Tbilisi itself was not the best place to raise two little sons alone. I had to work and take care of my children at the same time. There was no gas, no running water, no electricity. It was really hard and the cost of living through that period was high but, we survived.

My husband is an adventurous person ready to go to any country to fulfil any mission. He is also one of the best analytical thinkers and a connoisseur of international politics – the author of two books on US Foreign Policy. However, he is completely defenceless and helpless when it comes to everyday life, like paying taxes or utility bills, or simply cooking. Of course, he could have mastered all of this, but I tried not to let him do that. This may sound a bit weird, but I am happy to blame Georgian culture – in my understanding, my husband should devote his life and energy to what he has chosen as a profession, and I should be his support in the background. Just as a note: I do not even try to take this daily life burden off my shoulders; that is impossible, as I am happy, and it is how my life is run.

Being the wife of a diplomat is a huge responsibility as this means you devote your life to the person you love and at the same time to your homeland, the interests of which your spouse serves. And it was so pleasant and rewarding when, after all my efforts, I unexpectedly got from my husband the most remarkable Christmas gift in the form of the following poem:

To My Wife
When I was little I dreamt of Britain,
It was the El Dorado of my life,
I read about it, all that was written,
And chose an English-speaking wife.

True, the dreams come true, I came to Britain
Not only once but even twice,
Both times accompanied by that beautiful girl
My priceless English-speaking wife.

Time ran like a deer since life in Britain
Was so incredibly nice
Now I'm leaving for home, happy and sweetened,
Thanks to my honeyed wife.

Since the nature of God is wholly threesome
Shall I come to Britain thrice?
That is a good question – I will put it tomorrow
To my bright-eyed wife.

I hope sharing my experience will help others to better understand the challenges of the life of the family of a diplomat, in a new country of posting or back at home. Marrying into the diplomatic life is a courageous step. Any kind of a life is a combination of hard work and happy chance but, in addition to this, being part of a diplomatic family requires you to be the most flexible, adaptive, patient and loving person in the world. So be industrious, creative and intellectually curious and never put your personal ambitions aside, improvise a lot and you will succeed as a Spouse, a Wife and a Mum!

10 One Foot in Two Shoes: Being a Diplomat and a Diplomat's Wife

Olga Lucia Lozano

It is springtime in 2018. I am 53 years old. I am in a plane going to Taipei to visit my twenty-one-year-old son, who is doing his last semester at a French university. My husband is living in Chile, and my siblings are living in Colombia.

I am a happy woman. I have been a diplomat in my own right; I have been the wife of a diplomat; and at the moment I am both of these at the same time. I will tell my story as a way to thank God for the international life I have been living, with all its changes of direction, and to show that uncertainty itself can be a blessing.

I was born in a country with coasts on the Pacific Ocean and the Caribbean Sea, with three mountain chains, many rivers, and part of the Amazonian forest. I studied in a school founded in Spain by a priest dedicated to helping poor people in Guadix, Andalusia. Even though I belonged to a middle-class family in Colombia and thus went to a school with very high academic standards, my education was not bilingual, and at school I learned only the basics of English, so that I have had to spend the rest of my life learning more.

I remember my arts lessons with great emotion: my teacher Celine changing slides in her old projector, its strong lamp as warm as a heater, and my heart beating faster as I looked at the Parthenon or the Egyptian Pyramids. If it is true that we live our lives according to resolutions that we have made, I could say that it was within the four walls of that classroom, during those afternoons more than forty years ago, that I first dreamed of travel.

As a teenager, I watched *The Paper Chase*, an American TV series set in Harvard Law School: the unforgettable Professor Kingsfield; Mr Ford, a millionaire;

and, of course, Mr Hart with his red hair, the first-year law student who was the lover of Mr Kingsfield's daughter. My mother thinks that I studied law because she consulted an expert in vocational guidance who suggested it, but I think that the second resolution of my life was made watching *The Paper Chase*.

I went to the University Mayor de Nuestra Señora del Rosario, a traditional law school in Bogotá, founded in 1653. I was disappointed that, because of the influence of the Napoleonic Code in our law, we did not study based on cases, like Mr Hart did. Nor did I find Professor Kingsfield, although, as one of those wonders in life, my 'Introduction to Law' professor revealed the philosophy and theory of our legal system. When I finished law school in 1987, I started my career with an investigation of customs difficulties in donations for technical cooperation. Later, I studied financial law, and I studied English in Folkestone, a small English town.

I belong to a generation in which it is a privilege for a woman to become a professional. I thought that I had to choose between kids and a career, and I chose a career. I worked hard and was lucky to enter the field of foreign trade at a time when I had the chance of building a professional future. In the nineties, I was in charge of a project created by the Minister of Foreign Trade in Colombia, in which I collaborated in the implementation of the initial policies as well as in international negotiations. After this job, I worked at the Presidential Office, and was working there when I decided to have a child. I was thirty-one-years-old and felt I was not going to find my place in the world if I kept having my profession as my main purpose.

When Camilo was born in 1997, he changed my life. Since that moment, I have been taking decisions based on my roles as a mother and a wife, which I have placed at the core of my life. When he was a baby, I worked as a private consultant with a very flexible schedule. Later on, when a friend of mine was appointed Minister of Foreign Trade, she offered me a position in the ministry; maybe the only post I have held that has allowed me to have a normal schedule. Above all, since I was in charge of administrative issues, I did not have to travel abroad.

In 2000, an opportunity arose for me to be appointed to Geneva, Switzerland, to work in the Colombian Permanent Mission to the World Trade Organization. It was a great professional opportunity for me, but it was also a great challenge because my son was only three-and-a-half-years-old. I cannot say that our decision to accept that opportunity caused the end of my first marriage, but it was certainly a very big challenge to move to another country where only one of the spouses would have a job.

Eventually, though, I met a Chilean diplomat who is now my husband, and I had to be the one to follow his steps, to change my plans, or rather, to adjust them, in order for us to build a life plan together. At that time, I was forty-two-years-old, with professional achievements and a child; life had already given me great satisfaction, so I made the decision to build a life next to my current husband. I focused on a personal project of a life that privileged the companion woman instead of the professional one. I have to admit that, having been in the opposite position, I have to avoid thinking of myself as a victim asking for compensation for the enormous effort this relationship has demanded from me.

This difficult period of adjustment to my new life was garnished with wonderful trips: a cruise through the Baltic; Ireland; the land of the author of Heidi; a taste of the floating islands off the South of France; the farewell party for friends in Provence; and the lunchtimes we spent in Lyon. I travelled several times a year to Colombia, not only for work but also to spend time with my family and to see friends who, fortunately, I have kept in spite of the distance. Nowadays, they are one of my greatest treasures.

Later, we moved to Chile, the country of my husband, and it was even more difficult to adjust there. Not only was it hard to make friends, but when my son was a teenager, he wanted to finish his education in Colombia, so he went to live with his father. Having built my life around Camilo's daily routines, I was very lost, though I flew from Santiago to Colombia every six weeks. I decided to study regulation and competence at the university. I also taught in the Diplomatic Academy and in Adolfo Ibanez University, and wrote a chapter of the first book on World Trade Organisation (WTO) law in Spanish.

In 2012, my husband stayed in Chile while I lived in Colombia because I accepted a job for one year with the Colombian Ministry of Foreign Trade. Later on, we moved to the United Kingdom together when he was posted there. As is evident, the search in life never ends; we never stop looking for our place in the world, and we always want to build a better one.

London was like a second chance. I had been in that city as a student and dreamt of living there, so it was very exciting, and from the first day I decided to reinvent myself. I worked in a very small store as a saleswoman for some months. I then became a volunteer in Westminster Cathedral and also for a homework club in Paddington, where I helped the children of immigrants. For eighteen months, I was also a care worker.

I met very special people while in these roles, not only colleagues but also smart and very sweet girls and boys from immigrant families. I felt very comfortable with them. I felt that I shared with them this feeling of not belonging, this idea that we are in a beautiful and interesting place, but it is not our home.

The little story of my life starts with me as a diplomat with a husband who accompanies me to my post in Switzerland and takes an unexpected turn with the divorce. It continues with me as the wife of a diplomat, who then follows her husband to Chile and later on to London. As I write this chapter, I am a Vice Minister of Foreign Trade for Colombia, living in my country again, although my diplomatic husband still lives in London.

This chance to be Vice Minister arrived when my son was going to live six months in Asia and my husband was appointed to a position in his country, so I felt for the first time in many years that there was space for my own professional project.

I have always believed that the universe is a fair place and if you ask for something and fight for it, you will achieve what you want. This was my experience when I applied for my first job in international trade, and then many years later, when the Minister of Foreign Trade, Industry and Tourism gave me the opportunity to work for my country again.

I thank God for giving me so many opportunities and experiences, and my father who, because of the way he loved me, gave me the confidence to take risks. I have to admit that having taken so many risks makes me feel proud. It is precisely the fact of having lived my life from various angles that I would like to share in this chapter.

Challenges of a Diplomatic Woman with a Non-diplomatic Husband

I found it very difficult to adjust to a situation in which I was in charge of supporting the family while my husband was studying, even though I was very happy with my job. Working at the WTO took me right into the hub of international commerce, and allowed me to play two different roles simultaneously: I was an international negotiator and also the mother of a small child. I remember taking Camilo with me to meetings in the evening.

My husband travelled to Geneva with us but could only stay for forty-five days at first. During that short period, we had to find a house to rent and a school for Camilo. Fortunately, we managed. Public schools in Switzerland go from 9:00 to 11:30, and in the afternoon the schedule is from 13:30 to 15:00. There are no classes on Wednesdays. This was very inconvenient since I had to be in my office from 9:00 to 13:00 and from 15:00 to 18:00. In the end, we were very lucky because we found a private school offering a school day starting as early as 8:00 with the possibility for the children to stay until 17:00. It also offered activities on Wednesdays.

I remember those first months as a Colombian civil servant in Geneva as a series of challenges: finding out where to get food; learning how to handle the washing machine in the cellar of our building using a card on which money was deposited; remembering that there was an exclusive lane for the bus; understanding the processes of a multilateral system, which made me seriously question modern developments. I have never experienced the need for multitasking skills so evidently.

Since it was not possible for my husband to stay in Geneva from the beginning, my youngest sister, who has always been a great support, came along during the first months to help me out. My family in Colombia was very worried about how my son would adapt to a new environment, and my sister's support was crucial. She drew for him a big clock illustrating the activities throughout the day. It showed his aunt taking him to school at 8:30, the times for classes, lunch, and most importantly, the time when she would pick him up from school. Those months were vital for the development of the strong bonds between my sister and my son, who adapted very easily. On the first day, his teacher told me that he was going to be able to communicate in French in three months and that I did not have to worry. He learned French exactly as I had been told. He also learned how to ski, a sport that I started later. His great adaptability was a big lesson for me.

I was fascinated by the diversity of his classroom. It was like the United Nations. You saw people from all over the world getting together. Thanks to this experience, my son has developed great social skills and, above all, does not have the prejudices of the society in which I was born. Within this context, he learned to value the essence of people, regardless of the colour of their skin, their beliefs, who their parents are, where they live or their social status.

Those years, sharing with Camilo the discovery of a world full of possibilities, were very enriching. One of my most vivid memories is of a trip to Toscana, which Camilo and I ended up doing without his father because he had to stay to work on his post-doctoral studies. I remember making up a game in the Uffizi, a marvellous museum in Florence: when we entered each room, I noticed an object and asked my son, then aged five, to tell me which painting it was in. He looked at each painting until he found the object and was very happy about it. During this trip, I also established the rule that each of us would choose a restaurant during the day. That is, one time we ate where he wanted, and the next meal would be my selection. I have a beautiful memory of Camilo playing with pebbles in the middle of *la Toscana* with the cypresses in the background.

Living far away from your home country generates strong bonds with your children. I have often thought that the deep relationship, the soul connection, that I have with my son is due to our life in Switzerland. Had we stayed in our country of origin, our relationship would have been permeated by an extended family and it would have been different. Having spent so many special moments together has helped us to come close in a profound way and to develop an intimate relationship of complicity and fondness.

At the same time, during my years as an international civil servant, I gained great awareness of my status as a woman. Together with a Chilean friend, I used to organize meetings for women. I was not aware of the importance of such movements and the role gender was gradually gaining even in international commerce.

Those were very special years during which I unfolded in all aspects. I remember how proud I felt as I heard, 'Colombia, you have the floor', confirming that I was given the honour of talking on behalf of my country. At the same time, I had to deal with the guilt I felt for bringing my first husband into a situation in which he was so unhappy. I believe that, even though he made his own decision to focus on his studies, which was undoubtedly a benefit to his career, the fact that he was not working caused him great anguish, which in turn generated my feelings of guilt. In that sense, the fact that my husband was more actively involved in the housework and the care of our son caused me discomfort.

This conflict could occur in any marriage, but my diplomatic position added an extra spin, particularly as diplomatic spouses may be barred from work in some countries. I perfectly remember when, jokingly, people at receptions asked my ex-husband what it felt like to be a Prince Consort.

I think that this type of situation generates deep imbalances in couples because the roles that have been established from the beginning of married life are altered. Money management is modified and the concept of family, which is fundamental for couples, is undoubtedly lost. Without this support it is difficult to face so many challenges: a new job, in another language, in another country, finding a school, a house, and building a new life. If a strong relationship has not been built, these changes and challenges can end marriages.

Challenges of a Diplomat's Wife

The perception people often have of a diplomat's wife is that of someone dedicated to social life. The youngest of my nieces said a few years ago that she wanted to have my profession when she grew up, and when asked what her aunt's profession was, she said 'tourist'. Being able to travel around the world and to live in different countries does not mean that we go to fancy dinners every day, nor are we glamorous seven days a week. These social events are just a few. Most of the time is spent confronting everyday life and the challenges of starting all over again in another country.

As a diplomat's wife, I had no position or appointment of my own, so I faced the question of how to make a living. An old friend of mine, with whom I would form a business partnership, once said something I will always remember: if the Chinese are able to make shirts on ships, why shouldn't we be able to do consulting, you being in Switzerland and me in Colombia? For six years, we offered our consulting services for diverse projects using Skype. It was not easy because running a boutique company implied a constant search for clients and projects in the field of international commerce. To make things worse, my partner decided to have a child, so that our clients had a pregnant woman and a distant partner who spoke to them from the Swiss Alps via computer.

It would be unfair of me not to recognize that, as the wife of a diplomat, I have had many pleasures: spending time choosing the menu for a dinner party; enjoying having to choose a hat, and taking the time to carefully select flowers. I have travelled to many places and I have got to know more countries than I ever imagined. Undoubtedly, there are great advantages, and therefore I do not want to describe it as a life of suffering and regrets. Still, making the decision to take up a diplomatic role undeniably generates costs on a personal level.

One of the most difficult challenges in my case was transitioning from having an individuality of my own to being 'someone's wife'. This is because what brings us to a country and makes us part of a mission or an embassy is this circumstance of being married to a diplomat. In my case, because I was trying to set up a social network centred on my son's school, I also became 'someone's mother'.

It is precisely this quest to build a life as a part of another person's professional project that generates the greatest challenge of them all: trying to find a project of your own that goes beyond family. When you live in your own country, you have a social network of your own: your family of origin, your friends from school, your colleagues from work. When you move to another country, that community disappears, the husband acquires his own world at the office, the children go to school, and it is then that a diplomat's wife can choose to share those social networks or build a new one of her own.

During those years, my days started with taking Camilo to school. When I came back, I made myself some coffee and went into my office, a room in our apartment, which I left when it was time to fix lunch for my husband and me. In the afternoon, after picking up Camilo from school, it was time to talk with my team in Colombia. In this daily routine, Kalvin accompanied me, a beautiful Weimaraner, who in the morning lay on his carpet next to my desk and after lunch walked with me in a park nearby.

I had various close friends, the mothers of Camilo's schoolmates at the Ecole Primaire de Geneve, and then at the Spanish Section of the Lycée International de Ferney-Voltaire. We were very fortunate that an ambassador and his wife treated us as their family. Antonieta often picked Camilo up from school. Mario taught him how to make pizzas and talked to him about history and philosophy while they made them on Sundays. We often met friends for dinner, and during summer we spent Sunday afternoons at Lake Leman.

In Chile, without the network of mothers of Camilo's schoolmates and since I no longer belonged to the diplomatic circle, it was more difficult to make friends. Fortunately, we had a project to build a shelter in the snow, which used up a great deal of my energies and gave me great satisfaction. I very much enjoyed the skiing and spending time in the small town at the mountain, La Parva.

In London, I made friends among those I met through volunteering. I also took some courses, so I could work taking care of two ladies with Down's syndrome, a third with autism and a fourth with mental health problems. In my care worker role, I found what I was looking for: a place in the world to be useful and feel part of something, to develop new skills and another part of myself, a part that implied more than just my brain.

I remember one day attending a very formal ceremony in Westminster Abbey in the morning and in the afternoon cooking and ironing at my home-care job, happy to play different roles at the same time. I enjoyed worrying about what hat to wear for a very elegant and formal ceremony just as much as I enjoyed planning the menu for the dinner I would cook for the ladies with special needs, and, at the same time, being able to talk about Brexit or the situation of the WTO (with clients at my consulting firm/with people at diplomatic events I attended with my husband).

In previous times, women did not have to face this challenge of needing a project of their own because family was the mission and the purpose par excellence. In my case, I have maintained a continuous search that has led me to become a partner in a consulting company, to study at a university, to accept temporary jobs in my field of experience, as well as to care for people with special needs and to volunteer.

Another important challenge to be faced is the financial imbalance that arises when one spouse does not earn a living. The way that we dealt with this issue was with representation expenses that I had, which gave me freedom to cover daily costs. Even though my husband has been very generous, the fact that I stopped making pension contributions from a salary has generated a concern about my financial future. It is not easy for professional women to have to ask for money, and this has been one of the most complex issues of being a diplomatic wife.

I think that being the wife of a diplomat forced me to find a purpose in life earlier than most women, who are confronted with this at the age of retirement. Being the wife of a diplomat is like having to retire many times in one life. I have had to reinvent myself every time we have taken up a new post. Thanks to the existentialist approach I have had since I was a child, the experience of living in many countries has given me a lot of possible ways of making sense of my life.

I feel like a pilgrim searching for my place in life, asking myself many questions and taking many difficult decisions. But at the end, I am very happy because this long journey has made me a better person.

Challenges of a Professional Woman Living Far Away From Her Family

Working for the Ministry of Trade, Industry and Tourism, I had a job 24/7, meaning that even on weekends I had always a document to read, emails to answer or a report to write. I did not feel alone, maybe because I had my mother, brother and sister and their families with me, and friends from my school days. I really admire women with similar responsibilities, living with a husband and kids to take care of, because I find it very difficult to have energy for all of this.

Lessons

Without uncertainty, I wouldn't have learned much of what I will set down here; to learn that even uncertainty can be a blessing is the first lesson.

I have assembled many suitcases and have settled down several times. Today, I consider material things to be more ephemeral, and I attribute significantly less value to them.

While it is true that objects are magical in the sense that they remind you of a moment, bringing back a memory of a special family member or friend, they are still mere objects that make no difference; what does make a difference is people.

I have learned to enjoy every moment because I have learned that there are people that we will never see again or with whom we do not have the chance of having another cup of coffee.

It is also clear to me that places do not make people happy, that we carry our sorrows and joys and that it is our attitude that makes the difference; changing from one hemisphere to another or switching continents does not change who we are.

Likewise, knowing different cultures makes one less judgmental and more understanding. There is something wonderful about living abroad: it is precisely the search for our identity, the wonderful journey to the core of our being, that will, in the end, reveal to us who we are. Maybe we would not be confronted with these challenges had we stayed in the comfort of our own countries.

On this road through several countries, with so many experiences, it has become clear to me that life is a pilgrimage and that we grow as we walk through our days. The fact that we leave so many things and people behind has also taught me that life is a path of detachment.

Changing from one country to another has made me ask myself what my essence is. What is my mission? What is my purpose? Having to reinvent myself several times has made me inquire about what is important. When you change your landscape, your culture and your reality, you gain awareness, and it is easier to ask yourself 'what for?'

As a result of these inquiries, today I know more about who I am. I can distinguish between my circumstances and my essence. I know that what defines me is not a certain position or a job but my ability to communicate with people, what I bring to the table and my commitment to build a better world.

There are also great teachings in this life of changes. The vulnerability that we feel makes us aware of what little control we have; we are leaves flying through the wind in the hands of God. But at the same time, I have experienced the wonderful satisfaction of following my heart and my intuition in my decisions, rather than performing a careful cost-benefit analysis.

I am convinced that happiness is not a place, a person, a job, a specific circumstance. It is a clear decision to regard what is going on as an opportunity. I have learned that there is a mission in every moment of our lives, we cannot miss a moment or a chance to tell people what we have learned, and we must learn from everyone we meet.

Since it is my conviction that as a woman I have the mission to make a better world, in my work I have been trying to put all my intuition, my female perspective and my way of being a mother into taking care of the people who work with me. I am certain that our role in this world is to carry out our mission while keeping our essence, our identity.

Modern society must solve the problem that has been caused by the new role of women. In this scenario, I consider diplomatic wives to be outstanding because of being connected with a historical role, while at the same time they function as human beings who take care of their families, for which they are the central pillars, and who are able to assume their personal development as a second priority.

The world needs people who are able to be the central pillar for families and the support of the professional careers of others. But at the same time, we need husbands and wives able to understand the value of this kind of commitment. We also need for ministries of foreign affairs around the world to look after their civil servants, who are a key part of their teams abroad.

There is an urgent need to develop policies to support the members of these teams, giving them mental-health assistance, coaching them to seek alternatives and to find positive tools to face their challenges. There are institutions in charge of foreign affairs that are facing difficulties in finding diplomats because the partners of qualified candidates are not willing to sacrifice their professional careers.

I do not know now if I am going to move again from Colombia to another country. I do not know where I will live when I retire. I do not know if I will live again in the same city where my son will be, but I know that, thanks to the circumstances that I have had to overcome and all the experiences that I have accumulated, I have the tools in my bag to find my place in the world.

My son's drawing, 5 years old (casa in Italy, maja in Latvia, home in the UK)

11 Home, Casa and Maja: Language and Identity in a Trilingual Family

Monica Pavese Rubins

> *'γλῶσσα τύχη, γλῶσσα δαίμων'*
> *('The tongue is luck, the tongue is destiny')*
> **Plutarch, Morals**

My experience as a diplomat's spouse touches two countries – Sweden and the United Kingdom – and the two experiences could not have been more different.

In Sweden, I worked at the Italian Embassy as I am Italian. I met my Latvian husband in Stockholm, too, and decided to abandon everything to follow him to a new post, which could be highly beneficial for his career. I did not expect it would be so hard; I arrived in the United Kingdom naïve and full of expectations.

In London, I was not only an expat, but for the first time I felt like an outsider. I did not belong to anything anymore. I was not in Italy, where I grew up surrounded by family and friends, nor in Sweden where I was born, a well-known environment with family friends and new friends, where I had an interesting job and a good command of the local language. In London, I did not have a job, I knew just a couple of people, my level of English was quite poor, and I found the British system completely different. I was a spouse of a diplomat at the Embassy of Latvia, but I was not a Latvian citizen; I was the only foreign-born diplomatic spouse at the embassy, and I could not speak Latvian properly. That meant I was not fully included in the Latvian community in London, either, as the Latvian language still plays a strong role in the identity of Latvians for historical reasons.

Family Languages and Identities

Our diplomatic family has a mix of different identities, languages and citizenships. My mother tongue is Italian, but I am fluent in English, French and Swedish. My husband's mother tongue is Latvian, but he is fluent in English and Russian. My son's native languages are Italian, Latvian and English. The common language I share with my husband is English, but it is Italian between my son and me, and mostly Latvian between my husband and our son. Actually, my husband speaks constantly to him in Latvian, and Vittorio answers him mainly in Italian.

My husband has a clear Latvian identity with a Soviet background as he grew up in Latvia when his country was still part of the Soviet Union. My son, Vittorio, has both Italian and Latvian citizenships, but I would say that he is an Englishman as he was born in London and has experienced daily life and society only in Britain. Me? That is a bit more complicated. I was born in Sweden to an Italian family (academics, non-diplomats), but I grew up in Italy. At a certain point, my studies led me to France, where I got my PhD in history. Afterwards, I married in Latvia, and I gave birth to my child in the UK.

All my life, I, a foreign-born Italian citizen who moved back to my parents' home country as a child, have questioned myself about my identity. At present, I would say that I feel fifty percent Italian, twenty percent Swedish, twenty percent French, five percent Latvian, five percent English. But these percentages have constantly changed throughout my life according to my movements in the world. Every time I go back to Italy after a long time, I notice some changes, but most probably it is just me who mutates while abroad.

When you leave a place, you always lose something, but you also gain something new. In 2010, when we moved to London, different accents and pronunciations increased the force of the impact, starting on the first day of flat hunting when we could not properly sustain a conversation with the Cockney or the Scottish letting agents. We did not know that the sound *th* could become *f* or *v* in London. All slang was completely beyond our comprehension. We were also so used to the American accent from Hollywood films that the British one sounded completely unfamiliar. It took seven years to adjust and to learn the language here properly. Now I have become accustomed, and I love British received pronunciation.

With time abroad, I have discovered my homeland and the easiness of my own language, too. When I go back to Italy, I appreciate that my country has so many natural beauties. I grew up in Turin (in the north-west), which is surrounded by a wonderful crown of mountains. I can sit in front of the majesty of the Alps and stare for hours now. When I lived there, I did not notice them. Living abroad has also helped me understand what it means to be part of a community of people. When I walk around in my district in Turin, I can recognize the same faces that I have known since my childhood, even if I do not know the individuals personally.

After living places where you create your friends and acquaintances from scratch, you realize what having some family roots means. I have found them in my grandparents' small rural village near Asti. There, I can go around freely, talking in my first language, and no one will question why I am there and where I come from. My family house has been there for generations; my grandfather and father were born in that house and the people in the village have seen me growing up during my school holidays. Some cousins still live there; the family tomb where my grandparents are resting in peace is there. Some deep roots bind me to that place. There, people still call me by my family's nickname in the local dialect (*Tamagnina*), and some elderly villagers save the memory of my weird great-grandfather Tamagno, a bohemian free spirit who, at the beginning of the twentieth century, used to appear and disappear from home from time to time in order to vagabond around the neighbouring hills, to sing his own compositions and to flee from daily routine. He used to define himself as a 'small bird of the world' (*uccellino del mondo*). I can recognize in him something genetically related to me. My ancestral village gives me an overwhelming sense of identity and belonging.

The Challenges of a Diplomatic Spouse Whose Diplomat has a Different Citizenship and Language

Diplomatic and other expat families routinely juggle two cultures at a time, but if spouse and diplomat come from different cultures to begin with, the problems multiply.

My situation allows me to travel; get to know different realities; meet new, interesting people and be immersed in other cultures. But some aspects of my life are not easy, for example, any chance of continuing my career. My Latvian is not sufficient for me to volunteer at my husband's embassy, though I took some courses in the Latvian language at the University of

Stockholm. I have only lived in Latvia for three months overall, and I feel the linguistic barrier prevents me from fully integrating into my husband's country. Some cultural clashes occur at times, too. Speaking and thinking in another language means having to process information in another way. Sentence structures differ in Italian and Latvian. When the native language interferes, it can result in inconvenient misunderstanding.

My husband's life in Italy has instead become easier and easier over the years since he can understand and speak fairly good Italian now. I recognize that he has been more encouraged by my family and friends to try and experiment with his language skills. Italians are generally very keen to make foreigners feel comfortable in their language efforts. A native Italian would usually understand the meaning of a sentence even if the pronunciation, grammar and construction were completely wrong, or even if a non-native speaker were to pronounce just the roots of the Italian words without endings. If you decide to speak Latvian, you need to be very precise with your sounds and pronunciation in order to be understood.

Foreign-born spouses can face even more challenges with the arrival of a baby. In my case, I decided to devote myself fully to my child until he was at least three-years-old and to enjoy intensely the wonderful, priceless experience of being a mother. I also knew that I would be the only one who could teach him proper Italian, my mother tongue, so I put all my commitment and dedication into it.

Our family is constantly travelling among three countries (the two countries where our families live and the country where we are posted). It is very enriching to be fully immersed in another language and culture with different traditions and historical backgrounds, but you risk, after many years of this, becoming quite rootless. I feel like a tumbleweed, the plant of the desert that detaches from its stem and rolls constantly with the wind.

Starting Over From Scratch
I have always been a very independent person, working, studying and sustaining myself. Before moving to London, my professional life was fully engaged, working at the Scientific Office of the Embassy of Italy in Stockholm, even managing the office alone for over a year during the vacancy of the Scientific Attaché. I deeply loved writing scientific articles and reports, organising workshops, promoting an Italy bursting in sciences and

technologies in order to offer a different image of my country, commonly perceived just as a place of fun, sun, seaside, amusing food and wine, art, archaeology and fashion. So, I can understand my husband's desire to represent and promote his country abroad.

When I decided to follow my husband and to leave everything behind, I felt I lost my position in the world. When I went with my husband to an event, some people would not interact with me after they realised that I did not have a business card to exchange; it seems that a business card with a name and a position makes a big difference in this society, more than a person standing there in the flesh.

It is not rare to meet people who tell me, 'For me, it's important to work' or 'For my wife, the job is very important', implying that I must not like to work. I even got this reaction from someone I have known since I worked in Sweden, whose manner towards me changed the very day I became a diplomatic spouse in the United Kingdom.

It took me more than a year to understand the local system. Volunteering is the key in the United Kingdom, where people respect those who offer their time for free. It is socially useful, and it provides the opportunity to improve your knowledge of the language and of the local society. I volunteered at the Museum of London and the British Museum. I also immersed myself again in historical studies and research, which I could only do in my spare time when I was working. My passion could finally become my duty, while I improved my language skills. I published several articles and a book. After six years, I received my first public recognition in London, when I was elected as a Fellow of the Royal Historical Society.

It is very important to learn the local language properly, as proficiency is essential to find a job. A diplomatic spouse, as an outsider, has to be very flexible and extremely adaptable. They need to love travelling and be willing to reinvent themselves all the time. They should listen to the people, observe the local community and be able to take all it can offer.

When we arrived in London, we had to switch to a new life system overnight. From the relaxing quiet of human-scale Stockholm, where I was at my ease with the Swedish language, we moved to the big metropolitan centre of London. It took a few years to build a network of new friends and acquaintances, but we succeeded. Our son was born here, and we know now how to integrate ourselves into this complex reality.

A good tip is to start by getting a picture of the local system. You might join a club or attend some courses. I attended English classes where I could improve my language skills, meet nice people and open new horizons. Surprisingly, I learned something about my mother tongue, too. I learned that the strong accent characteristic of Italians speaking English is connected to a completely different approach to articulating the words – which in English occurs towards the back of the mouth, while Italians tend to pronounce the words at the teeth. Also, all syllables in Italian are pronounced with the same weight, while in English one syllable is more stressed than the others. A word that is written exactly in the same way in Italian and English may result in two completely different words when spoken: an Italian BÁ-NÁ-NÁ is an English ba- NÁ-na. I had to learn a different way to pronounce every single letter of the alphabet, too, but between my volunteer work and my studies, my English became good enough to express myself in a globally spoken language to reach a wider public with publications and speeches for my historical research.

When I finished my study of English, I took advantage of free business and economics classes. Within a few months, when I met decision-makers at those VIP events where people used to walk away from me, I could hand them my business card, complete with impressive job title. I was the International Development Business Director of an excellent Latvian design company that wanted to enter the British market. It was very exciting to engage in a completely new career, where I could apply my fresh business studies. The core was constantly networking, meeting the decision makers and having a high position on my business card, in order to offer original design services from an unusual country, located between West and East Europe, Scandinavia and Russia. Moreover, the fact I came from Italy, a country world famous for design, helped to sell Latvian design services in the UK. An Italian representing a foreign design company was indeed a positive. After just four months, I created the first fruitful contacts, and after six months the company could submit their first tender to a British partner. After one year, I managed to take on the negotiations and sign an exclusive partnership contract with a world-famous design company.

I have learned the hard way, so I have been very keen, as the President of the Diplomatic Spouses Club in London in 2018, to share my experience and to help other newcomers to settle down.

Language Building of a Cross-Cultural Child in a Globetrotting Multilingual Family

The issues are even bigger in a diplomatic family with children. One is the question of the development of language. I really wanted my child to be trilingual as it was a good way to develop his three identities and cultures.

Observing other multilingual families, diplomatic and not, I noticed that sometimes children refused to use their parents' mother tongue, and some children did not even know their father's or mother's language. I met many inspiring children who were perfectly bilingual or trilingual, even speaking without strong accents. I believed that a full knowledge of each language would allow Vittorio to go deeper into his interpersonal relations and to understand fully the society and culture of both sides of his family. The benefits and challenges of growing up as a cross-cultural child are well analysed by David Pollock in *Third Culture Kids*, about children who spend a significant period of their developmental years in a culture outside their parents' passport cultures (Pollock, 2009).

I really wanted my son to learn all our languages so he could take advantage of all of the benefits Pollock describes. Every time we have moved from one place to another, I have immersed him in the local education system. But I am aware that changing nurseries presents fewer difficulties than attending different school systems. Now that Vittorio has started primary school in London, the next time we move will certainly be more problematic. How will he face the challenges stemming from deep changes, such as school systems, friends, environment?

Many diplomatic families choose to follow a more homogeneous path, which could be, for example, boarding schools, which did not seem an option for us as we aimed to stay together. Some choose to send their children to, say, a French school or an international school in every country to which they are posted. I know a very successful diplomatic family where the father is Italian, the mother is Latvian, the children attended a Russian pre-school and kindergarten in Riga, and attended Russian schools wherever the family was posted abroad. Now they are perfectly trilingual (Italian–Latvian–Russian).

Home, Casa and Maja

Ever since my son was very small, I have tried to help him to face his difficulties with continually moving among three countries. I started from the very beginning to distinguish the three countries by using a different word to identify each of them: *home* in London, *casa* in Turin and *maja* in Riga. In this way, he could clearly identify each language and each place. In order to make him comfortable when moving around, I have always tried to recreate his own personal space with his own personal corners where he could find a sort of stability.

Vittorio became fluent in English at around two-and-a-half years. Before that, his language was what is termed telegraphic (sentences of two or three words) in a mix of Italian, Latvian and English. He started to speak a bit later than average, like many other bilingual and trilingual children. At one and a half, he could say around fifty words – though he knew each word in all three languages. For example, he would ask for *water-acqua-udens* or for *car-mashina-macchina*. His development was completely in line with that of monolingual children, who also should know about fifty words at that age, except that Vittorio racked up fifty words in three languages. My son's preschool and school have run smoothly, and his teachers have always been pleased by his good ear and skills in phonetics. He can probably reproduce a wider range of sounds than most children, too, as his three languages belong to three different linguistic groups: Germanic, Romance and Baltic.

When Vittorio started nursery for a few hours a week at eighteen months, his first language suddenly became English, followed by Italian and Latvian. Then, when he was two-years-old, we moved for three months to Latvia; Vittorio attended the local nursery, and his first language became Latvian, followed by English, and the weakest one was Italian. When he was three-years-old and we moved to Italy for a while, he did not speak much in public for the first month, but then his first language suddenly became Italian, followed by English and Latvian. When we moved back to London, Italian and English became more or less similar, and Latvian is still now his least favourite language. At present, at the age of five, when Vittorio dreams, I hear him expressing himself sometimes in English and sometimes in Italian (almost never in Latvian).

It is not an issue if a bilingual or trilingual child starts to talk later; that is just part of the process, especially when he or she has no older siblings. The sociolinguist Dr Patton O. Tabors talks about 'the silent stage' and suggests avoiding any kind of pressure to push a child out of his mutism as this would end up slowing down his linguistic development (1997: 43). When we met a new group of people or faced a new situation, Vittorio, at four, would stare around silently, not even answering if someone spoke to him. But when he was sure about which language to use, he would start to talk. I never pushed him to speak if he did not want to.

When my son was between one-and-a-half and two-years-old, he created strange mixes of words, like *bamba* for 'ball' (the Italian is *palla* and the Latvian is *bumba*), or he started sentences in one language and finished in another, like *Kur ir il mio bicchiere?* – where *Kur ir* in Latvian is 'Where is' and *il mio bicchiere* is 'my glass' in Italian). At four-years-old, his levels of Italian and of English were quite good. Sometimes, he used odd constructions or words; when he played chase with one Italian-Lebanese-English friend, he incorrectly used the word *cacciami* ('hunt me'), instead of *prendimi* ('catch me'), choosing an Italian word that sounds similar to the English one (*cacciami* for 'catch me'), but in Italian that sounds a bit strange. At other times, Vittorio and his friend compensated for a missing word by using English. Regarding such cases, Dr Abdelilah-Bauer talks about the 'lexical potpourri' created as children mix and borrow words from a variety of languages to compensate for gaps (2006: 50-56). Code-switching, which means alternating two or more languages while speaking, is in fact an integral part of multilingual behaviour, especially in the early stage of a language acquisition in bilingual/trilingual children (Fantini, 1987: 44).

Even while living in London, my son at five is indeed fluent in Italian, but he is making some mistakes when building sentences. I would not say his efforts are completely wrong, but they are not really correct. For example, he puts the adjective in front of the noun, where speakers of colloquial Italian usually prefer to put the adjective after the noun; he says *la mia bianca maglietta* ('my white t-shirt') instead of *la mia maglietta bianca*, which seems a very poetic form of Italian. In this case, he is using an English grammatical structure with an Italian adjective in front of an Italian noun.

Successfully Raising a Trilingual Child

When Vittorio was four-and-a-half-years-old, he was starting to use his language skills fruitfully; he could understand, talk and play in three languages with a wider range of peers and speak with Italian and Latvian relatives in their own languages. He could speak English and Latvian with his Guatemalan-Latvian cousin who lived in Scotland. He suddenly started making fun of mum and dad, because our pronunciation of English was not clean enough. As Dr Abdelilah-Bauer writes (2006: 55), my son understood that his words were part of three different languages and three different systems.

According to Dr Abdelilah-Bauer, when raising a multilingual child, the main tip for parents is to stick with their own mother language from the very beginning. In fact, the infallible method for developing each language separately is frequent contact with monolingual people, because it allows the child to better distinguish between the linguistic systems (2008: 57-59). Mother-tongue teachers and friends will teach them the second or third language correctly.

I have spoken to my son exclusively in Italian; my husband has spoken Latvian with him about half the time, because he was busy at work. Since he was four-years-old, Vittorio has also been going to the Latvian Sunday school in London, where he learns not only the language, but also the culture and the folklore, dances and songs. By contrast, he has learned English at the nursery, at school, at swimming courses, in the streets, in the shops, in the libraries and from Disney DVDs. We have scrupulously avoided talking to him in English because our incorrect pronunciation could have confused him. At his British primary school, he even started to learn his fourth language, French. He seemed immediately very interested in it, and he liked to repeat the French sounds he learned in class.

Now, his weakest language is Latvian, and he uses it when he is forced to, in the presence of people with whom he has just Latvian in common, or whenever he needs something from his dad. For a while, he also tried to make my husband give up using Latvian with him. When my husband started a conversation with him in Latvian, he would turn to me and ask, 'What did he say?' in Italian. Whenever my husband starts a conversation in Latvian, my child sticks to answering in Italian. After a while, my husband switches to Italian, too.

Now Vittorio prefers Italian at home. He does not mind if my husband and I speak English to each other, but he cannot accept us talking to him in English. If my husband tries to speak English, Vittorio says, 'Please don't use this language'. Probably he perceives that there is some required minimum competence in a language, some level of error that should not be tolerated. He also does not speak English if I am present in the room. I always encourage him to switch languages with people who do not speak Italian, and if I leave the room, he suddenly turns to English or Latvian.

An interview with my child (at the age of five)

Today I'd like to ask you something about home (London), casa (Turin) and maja (Riga). Which do you feel to be your homeland? London, Riga or Turin?
All three are homes for me.

We have been living for a while in London, Riga and Turin. Which place do you prefer?
London.

Why?
Because here I go to school. I play with my best friends. I play football here.

Which place do you like less?
Riga, because I have less toys there.

You have been in a nursery in all three countries. Which one did you like more and which one less?
More the nursery in London because I could always play at the open air. Less in Turin because I couldn't play outdoors. I liked Riga's nursery because I loved the porridge they made for breakfast and the way I played there.

What did you feel when we had to move for a while to live in Turin and leave London?
I was unhappy. But I still like to play in the bathtub in Turin's home.

Did you feel happy to come back to London?
Yes

Why?
Because we were again together, me, Mummy and Daddy.

Which language do you like more?
Italian and English. With Mum I speak Italian and with friends I speak English at school. But with my Italian friends at school, we speak Italian.

And with Dad?
French

French? But Dad cannot speak French...
That's why I'd like to teach him.

If you could choose, where would you like to live?
I'd like to live in the grandparents' countryside house [in Italy, nearby Asti].

Why?
Because I'd like to have a dog. In the countryside, I could have a dog.

Farewell from my pre-schoolers at Kampung Kids, Karta.

12 How to Make Friends, Make a Difference and Make Sure Those at Home Don't Forget You

Emilia Atmanagara

I have been on my second posting as the spouse of a diplomat, this time in London, for almost three years now. I could highlight many wonderful aspects of the diplomatic life; equally, at times I have felt invisible and struggled to keep my own identity. Some people would think I had no identity apart from my spouse's. I want to break down the stereotype that a spouse just follows the diplomat around the world from post to post without a personal life or individual identity, living in a world of parties and luxury, not aspiring to do or to be anything more. You will find other educated women with their own interests, some of whom will become lifelong friends; you can maintain your own identity while on post; and you can remain connected to the people you left behind in your home country.

I am the Indonesian-born spouse of a diplomat from Australia. In addition to having enjoyed two wonderful overseas postings, I have my own successful career in Canberra as a senior civil servant. My roles have been varied and I intentionally moved departments to improve my skills as a public servant as well as my understanding of government policy and processes. I also spent some time working as a departmental liaison officer working in a minister's office so I could understand 'the other side' and feel more accomplished as a public servant. Serving the public was a career that was challenging, interesting and rewarding. Reflecting on my career, I am satisfied with my choice and that the work I did made a difference.

My children have made me a very proud grandmother of six, plus my diplomat has an adult son from a previous relationship, yet all of our postings were without children because my spouse became a diplomat late in life. As an adult, I feel, I have lived three lives: firstly, as a stay-at-home mum, which I loved; then as a single mum, struggling to balance work and family responsibilities; and, if you fast-forward to today, as the spouse of a diplomat, as a mother and a grandmother and, at the same time, as a civil servant. These diverse lives have shaped who I am today and provide the reason why keeping my own identity is so important to me.

Background and Early Life

My parents grew up during the Dutch occupation of Indonesia and because their parents were high-ranking public servants, they were educated in Dutch-speaking private schools until, during the Second World War, the Dutch left Indonesia and closed the schools. Then they continued their studies in local schools where they learnt English. They also spoke Bahasa Indonesia and Sundanese (West Javanese Dialect). My father spoke Japanese (learned during the occupation) and they both studied German later in life.

My parents left Jakarta for Australia when I was two-years-old. Growing up, I spoke a mixture of Bahasa, Sundanese, Dutch and English, but as a child I always responded to my parents in English as it was the language I was most confident in speaking because I spoke it at school and with my friends. Dutch was my parents' preferred language if they did not want the children to know what they were talking about.

In her early twenties, my mother lived for seven years in France and Belgium with her sister and Indonesian-diplomat brother-in-law. This is when my mother studied French, aspiring to live in Europe and never return to live in Indonesia. Unfortunately, she was made to go home to marry my father, who had waited for her to come back. It was a different time for women of my mother's generation.

In Jakarta again, my mother married my father and had me, but was not happy as she preferred the European lifestyle of parties, weekends away and full-time study. Because of her language skills, she became the secretary to the French Ambassador. Later, they moved with me to Australia for my father to become personal assistant to the ambassador at the Indonesian Embassy in Canberra. They lived the rest of their lives abroad. While it was a shock initially as my mother had expected life to be just like her experience in Europe, they soon adapted to life without a nanny for me, a maid or a cook. Neither knew the first thing about cooking or cleaning but they soon learned and built a very good life for their family away from Indonesia. For that I am truly grateful! Life in Australia is very different; less crowded, better opportunities for education and job prospects. I think, though, that had I grown up in Indonesia, I would have had a good life, too. Being a diplomatic spouse in Indonesia I have had the experience of living in the country where I was born. It was also good to reconnect with family there and to get to know them more.

I feel I have roots in Indonesia and a strong sense of belonging, but it is not my home. In fact, my Indonesian cousins say that I do not act very Indonesian, which is not surprising given that I have spent most of my life in Australia, apart from accompanying my diplomat on his overseas postings.

Reflecting on Life as a Diplomat's Spouse
The experiences I have had on postings have been wonderful. Celebrating Queen Elizabeth II's birthday, and William and Kate's wedding in Jakarta at the British Embassy, and then attending the Queen's Garden Party at Buckingham Palace in London, as well as having the opportunity to travel in Asia and Europe, are some of the highlights. But, at times, these postings have included periods where I have been lonely, have been frustrated or have endured bouts of homesickness that have lasted for days and weeks.

And then there is the stereotype of a diplomat's spouse as someone living in a romantic world of fancy houses with maids and drivers, fashionable events and a life of caviar and privilege. In some countries you have access to all of this and more! Shopping expeditions, access to all the best hotels and restaurants, dressing up to attend events on national days, being invited to celebrations for royal weddings and birthdays – these are all fantastic experiences and certainly a lot of fun, but this is not reality for most people on posting.

There are still the everyday chores to do – the food shopping, cooking, washing and ironing. For example, while we are very much a couple and as such a team, I see my role as my diplomat's support, so he can do the job he was assigned. While on posting, I have more free time, so it falls to me to handle tasks we would routinely share at home, such as paying the bills, dealing with the real estate agent and the accountant and anything to do with setting up a home and its maintenance. It is a role I take as seriously as he takes his job.

I try to put the postings into perspective by remembering that a posting is usually three years and when we go home it is back to reality. For me, this means going back to a job in the public service and everything that goes with working full-time.

The life of a diplomatic spouse has given me amazing opportunities and experiences, but had I wanted to further my career in the Australian Public Service, being a diplomat's spouse would not be the path I would take.

My Diplomat

Having a good relationship with your diplomat is the foundation for success at post (and at home). I have seen couples who come to a post with relationship issues thinking that the move will fix their problems, who have then found that being so far from their usual support networks exacerbates the trouble.

I am very lucky. My diplomat is sensible, calm, kind and generous; we are different, personality-wise, but share the same values, principles, and sense of humour. Before he accepts a posting we talk through everything, including the job he will be doing and its impact on life for me. We talk about money, as one of my issues is not being financially independent. My diplomat feels that supporting him at post is a job in itself, and he leaves it up to me to decide whether I will get another job on top of that.

The current posting in London involves a lot of overseas travel for him. The upside means that sometimes I travel with him and go to countries I probably would not visit; the downside is that I can find myself on my own for long periods. It can be a hard slog, especially on weekends, and if I have not yet made local friends. I prefer not to bother my diplomatic spouse friends on the weekend as that is their family time. I can fall back on technology and contact family and friends back home to help keep me sane and not feeling lonely. My diplomat keeps in touch with me when he is travelling, too, as it can also be lonely for him.

Settling In at Post

If you let it, moving to a new country can be overwhelming. I cannot stress enough how important good communication is. Before we leave, even before my diplomat applies for the posting, I ask lots of questions and think about what I might like to do while we are overseas: work, study, volunteer. It is important for us to do our research on the city and country before we pack up and go.

We even research accommodation together and the best location to live that suits both our needs. There are important requirements for him, like proximity to work and availability of public transport if he is not provided with a car or driver. At our current post, I needed a place I could feel safe and secure, close to amenities, shops and restaurants. I did not want to be isolated out in the suburbs without a car or people around while he was away. The good thing about being posted to London was that he had travelled there regularly, so he was very familiar with the different areas. We chose a city district together before we arrived in the UK. At some posts, you do not have a choice, but that is okay, too. It is important to be flexible and be up-front about any reservations you may have. It is so important to talk!

Once you know where you will be living, you still have to rethink the basics – even food. Your favourite brands from home may not be available. Often, you can find a local alternative. My motto: Try it – you might like it! Eventually, you will work out where to source the staples that you already like, and you will come to love new foods that you will miss when you go back home. In Jakarta, I learnt to cook my favourite Indonesian dishes from scratch, like beef rending and gado gado, instead of using pre-made spice mixes. As my maid was not a good cook (she was a nanny) I gave her lessons and, luckily for us, she was an excellent student and made everything, from Indonesian, Australian and Thai to Italian. Her baked goods were delicious. I also attended a cooking class at the Marriot Hotel and had a great time cooking, as well as sampling dishes.

In London, I watched Mary Berry, Tom Kerridge and Jamie Oliver cooking shows and now I have a repertoire of go-to dishes, like Mary's Mississippi Mud Pie, Tom's miso glazed salmon and Jamie's pasta dishes. Food shopping in a new country can provide hours of activity and is a good way to explore your new city when you have not yet made friends. Visitors from home often come bearing gifts of things you cannot get abroad. Internet shopping is a wonderful thing. In short, you can learn to adapt. We are grateful for the wonderful fresh produce available overseas, and experimenting with products that we do not get back home. Food shopping at post increases your knowledge of the preferred foods of certain cultures. It is a great way to add to your repertoire and to mix food cultures to create your own dishes. The range of fresh food markets back home is limited, and I regularly lament to family and friends how I will miss my daily shopping at Borough Market in London and how shopping for fresh produce at the supermarket will not be the same. It is not only the produce that I will miss but the whole experience – the ambience, chatting to my fruit man, asking the Turkish Deli lady what her favourite olives are, the divine smells emanating from the French bakery stall and buying fresh, Cornish, line-caught mackerel from my favourite fishmonger.

When overseas, systems and processes are different to what I am used to in Australia. Health systems and navigating through the process of registering for health cover will try the patience of a saint. Working out the public transport system in a big city and getting mobile phones will provide hours of fun! Not having the language can also be a challenge. Even if you are sent to an English-speaking country where it is assumed that you will not have language worries, in large cities the absence of communication barriers does not automatically lead to a trouble-free transition to your new life. English is my everyday language at home, but in the UK some words are used differently. I can think of a few funny examples. When we moved into our apartment, I told the agent that I had fixed our bed. She was shocked as she thought the bed was broken, when in fact I meant that I had made the bed. The British do not say pants; it is trousers because pants mean underpants. The first time I asked for an eggplant and rock melon at the fruit and vegetable stall I was told I wanted an aubergine and a cantaloupe.

After a while things fall into place, though some say – and I agree – that it can take up to a year to feel settled at post. It is good to compare notes with other spouses. By sharing experiences, you quickly learn that you are not alone and that your problems are not unique. It can also help spouses avoid some of the frustrations that I experienced and vice versa. By sharing, we often find ourselves in tears of laughter at how similar our experiences have been.

While you are taking your first steps, though, whenever you achieve something overseas it will provide you with a wonderful story for your next dinner party. In Jakarta, my diplomat's first posting, we arrived with my Bahasa Indonesia language skills a little rusty. As a weekend outing, we took three of the grandchildren to a place where, for the payment of a modest admission charge, you can go 'fishing' and are guaranteed to catch fish. The grandchildren had a lovely time and caught masses of fish. I had not read the sign correctly so did not understand that you pay for your catch by the kilo, and get to take the fish home. It ended up being an expensive afternoon that, with the space of time, we laugh about now.

However, at times there were real tears at being unable to achieve easily what you expect to be the simplest of tasks, like registering with a GP in London, which took months. You cannot just go to the local surgery and make an appointment. You need to check whether the surgery accepts someone living in your postcode area – very simple, but only if information provided on websites and by GP receptionists is correct. To add to my frustration, no surgery uses the same form, so that meant completing multiple forms from scratch. After five attempts, the surgery that registered us was only minutes away on foot. I made a tearful call to my diplomat to say I had successfully registered for a GP and we went out to celebrate that evening. Getting things done overseas can be a real achievement. I am not sure that many of us at post actually think of it that way.

On our first posting, I was (very wisely) told that just because they do things differently in another country does not mean it is wrong. These words kept me grounded and helped me to accept that the country was not going to change – I needed to adapt and accept the way things were done in the new country. (Mind you, I had to keep repeating this to myself when things got hard.) With this revelation, settling in was easier (mostly) as I did not have unrealistic expectations – in fact, at times I learned not to have any expectations at all! What a relief to be able to go with the flow and not feel like you are pushing a very full wheelbarrow up a mountain. And what a delight it is when things go unexpectedly smoothly, and the outcome is way better than it would have been at home. We were so impressed that internet speed in Jakarta and London was far superior to what we had at home and on-line shopping in London for everything is a thing!

Being at post is different again for the diplomat. A diplomat is automatically part of a network, with a job and a purpose, somewhere to go and something to do every day and people to talk to! To be fair, they have to settle in, too – a new job, boss, colleagues, and staff, as well as a new country. So, the spouse and posted officer have something in common, which provides a chance to bond, to support each other and to enjoy the experience as a couple.

Setting Up a Network of Friends
My priority when starting in a new location is to establish networks with other spouses from my country so that I can feel connected to home. This can be difficult when there is not a structured opportunity to meet them. There is different support available for spouses at different posts,

depending on the size of the delegation, whether the country you find yourself in is English speaking and whether you have children with you. At one post you may have someone contact you before you arrive, as well as regular welcome and farewell get-togethers; at other posts this does not happen. The same goes for social activities for spouses; some posts are very active in this area and others are not. Also, while being an older spouse means there are no children to worry about, the upside of having children with you at post is the instant network you have through your children's schools and other parents.

My strategy is to take my own initiative and put in the time and effort to make it happen. I create my own new network. If my embassy has a Community Liaison Officer who doesn't get in touch with me, I get in touch with them, offering my contact details for them to pass to new arrivals. If all else fails, I ask my spouse to give my contact details to a new colleague's spouse. I have learned to try not to have any expectations and to be patient – this avoids too many disappointments when things do not go the way I want.

I also try to find a diplomatic spouse association of some kind so that I can meet spouses from other embassies to widen my circle of friends. In the UK, I was lucky enough to find the Diplomatic Spouses Club of London (DSCL). The DSCL has provided me with a network of peers who can empathise with my trials and joys. It has given me some lovely friends. Being part of the DSCL Committee afforded me the opportunity to contribute to the well-being of others, and it gave me a defined role while in London. I really enjoyed organising club events, whether cultural or informational activities, or just-for-fun coffee get-togethers.

In Jakarta, I was familiar with the city and had a ready network of family who I reconnected with seamlessly. My diplomat got to meet my extended family and I spent plenty of time getting to know them and learning about our family history. I felt at home in their company and discovered how different and yet similar life was for them. Most of my cousins around my age were working so I was able to meet up during their lunch break and the weekends, which meant long drives in traffic to their homes. Mostly, I loved hanging out with my mother's older sister, the one she went to live with in Europe, and my father's younger brother who was a retired officer in the military. One of the best times was when my mother came to visit around the time of her eightieth birthday. I organised a luncheon at a traditional

Sundanese restaurant and invited family to attend. It made my cousins and I so happy to see my mother and her siblings together and, as it turned out, it was for the last time. My mother, her sister and a brother have all passed away since then.

Throughout the adventures, compromises and challenges of life abroad, I built up a rich and interesting international network of friends for whom I will be forever grateful. Living in another country, and meeting and being exposed to people from different cultures, is a unique life, but unless you have lived it first-hand, it can be difficult to understand or relate to. Finding your own network of other diplomatic spouses can help. Some of the supportive people I have met on posting have become friends for life. They are people who have provided me with love, support, laughter and a lot of fun. They really understand everything about being a diplomat's spouse and are interested in who I am as an individual.

While moving from postings and back to your home country is unsettling and leaves you uncertain of whom you are, I found that I have become someone who can make a life anywhere in the world, handle situations outside my comfort zone and can make friends wherever I am.

Relationships and Communication – Remaining Visible to Those at Home
Relationships with those left behind can suffer when you are at post – especially friendships and connections with work colleagues. One benefit of being in the public service is that you can take leave without pay from your job while your diplomat is on a posting. When you come back, you have a job to go back to at the same level and salary.

One of the most important things for me in setting up in my new home is the technology to connect me with those I love; it is my lifeline. I cannot tell you how much I look forward to daily updates on life at home, so I feel connected and not so isolated and alone. A short message or a photo – anything from home is a treat. I have a few very close friends in Australia whom I have had for decades, and we always make the time and effort to communicate. Conversations with colleagues keep me informed of what is happening at work – good, bad and funny. It is also great when a colleague uses you as a sounding board; it makes me feel like I am still valued in a work sense.

One day without technology is one day too long. I often think about how hard it must have been during my mother and father's time when they only had mail to rely on. Even as a child, I remember writing to my grandparents and getting letters back, but having no memory of them is a huge gap in my life. Today's technology, though, means that I remain visible to my grandchildren, even if it is not exactly like being in the same room with them and being able to give them kisses and cuddles. I have great kids who contact me regularly, almost daily, even if it is just a quick message to say hello or just send an emoji. The older grandchildren have their own devices, which makes it easy to keep in touch with them, catch up on their news, swap funny selfies, jokes and stories, and be a part of their birthdays and special occasions. And the little ones used to open their laptop to see if I was in there – how funny and cute! They thought I lived in the computer; one of my grandsons often asked me to 'come to the other side'. Watching the grandchildren playing or having them ask me to show them our home and surroundings means that I can share their lives at home and share with them a little of life in a foreign country.

Sometimes, though, the grandchildren come to me or I visit them. Three of my grandchildren were very young when we left to go on postings, and one was born while I was overseas; while I regretted not being there for the birth, I was free to go home and spend six weeks getting to know her. I would not have been able to do that if I were living in Australia but working full-time. On my visits, I can help with the daily grind, like getting children ready for school and doing school drop-off and pick-ups, which I would rarely have time for if I were back home and working.

Twice during one three-year posting, I had a three-month visit from my daughter and her three children. This was invaluable time for all of us and a benefit of being a diplomat's spouse. This is also true for my spouse's family. His relatives have come to visit us, and the quality time we spent together makes us so much closer. We can share our favourite walks or restaurants and explore different parts of the country with them. For example, we have taken visitors to Taman Safari, a drive-through zoo in Bogor, West Java, not far from Jakarta. It is also the same with friends. During a visit to London, one of my close friends happened to be visiting during the Australian and New Zealand Army Corps (ANZAC) day commemorations and I was able to take her along to the laying of the wreaths at the ANZAC memorial, and to attend the service at Westminster Abbey, where Princes William and Harry, and Meghan Markle, were also in attendance. We have taken trips with family to beautiful parts of the UK, such as Devon, Cornwall, Sussex and Scotland.

I was worried that my grandchildren would not know who we were when we came home and that my relationship with them would be affected. Technology has certainly made it easier to be a constant in their lives. Staying in touch with work colleagues made my transition back to work easier as I was up to date with organisational changes and had information on the job I was going back to.

Leaving Behind Elderly Parents – Dealing with Feelings of Guilt
When we left for London, my mother was 85-years-old. It was a very hard decision, but in the end, I felt it was the right decision for me. Despite my guilt about leaving her, I knew that I would never stop one of my children from having a life, and that she would feel the same, so, with a heavy heart, I joined my diplomat. Before we left, I was fortunate enough to have six months leave from my job to focus on my mother's needs, during which I put into place a plan of activities for her four times a week to ensure that she had a social life. She lived with my brother and his family, and had my sister and my nieces, who were very supportive of her. There were also, of course, my children and their children, my mother's great-grandchildren, who visited regularly and kept her entertained and feeling loved.

When she became very ill, I was able to fly home to spend time with her and to work with my sister to find fulltime care for the final stages of her life. It was very difficult to leave her again, but the geriatrician and my family convinced me to go back to my life at post after two weeks.

While I was unable to visit mum in her final days or to attend her funeral (she was buried very quickly in accordance with her religious beliefs), I was able to see her and talk to her regularly via technology. I even managed to speak with her in her dying moments, after she had been unconscious for days. When she heard my voice for the last time she opened her eyes and smiled at me. Had I not been able to 'see' my mother regularly via FaceTime and at her final breath, I would have felt a sense of guilt for the rest of my life. In the end, I knew she was in a safe place and being well cared for to the end. On reflection, spending six months caring for her before we went to London was precious time.

Work-life Balance vs Climbing the Corporate Ladder

Being separated from family and not working at the first posting helped me realise how much more I missed my family than I missed my job.

When I first considered leaving my successful career to go on post, I earned a very good salary, enjoyed my financial independence, and was on a path to being promoted to a more senior role. I accepted high profile projects, which meant long hours, high pressure and little free time. At home, I was always checking my emails, my mind on the job, not at home, in the present, with my family. Thinking about it now, I was on a treadmill that I could not get off, or would not – my ego was influencing my career decisions. I got a lot of satisfaction from my bosses and peers giving me good feedback and, somehow, I thought that the work would not get done without me.

Then I followed my diplomat to post and – guess what? The work got done, the project was completed, everyone was happy, and I was not even in the country. Who would have thought it? People get on with the job, your staff and bosses adjust, and you realise that you are not indispensable.

At my first post, not having a job meant I had plenty of time to reflect, and I realised the real joy and happiness in my life came from my roles as partner, mother and so forth, especially grandmother, rather than from my career. My work gave me a sense of identity, independence, and responsibility, but the higher up the corporate ladder I moved, the more precariously my work-life balance would tilt towards my job. Realizing that money was no longer a driver for me (easy for me to say since our children are adults, we are debt-free, and my public-service status guarantees me a salary on my return), I decided that when I went back home and resumed working, I was not going to chase any more promotions.

I feel so blessed to have had the space to reflect and to re-adjust my priorities. Not worrying about being on the bottom of the promotions list when I got back has given me so much emotional freedom that I believe it helped me embrace my role as a diplomat's spouse even more at the second posting. I did not lose my identity by stepping out of my job for a while, I clarified it.

I Am Not Invisible – I Have a Place in the World
While I have made a decision on what I need from my career, I still want to have my own identity while at post. Once I have settled in, I need to occupy myself and my brain.

Initially, when you first arrive at post, some people only want to know what your diplomat does and where he or she (that is, you) fits into the hierarchy. This type of question, from people trying to work out the rank of your diplomat and whether you are worth being friends with, can become tiresome. I need to clarify that most spouses are not like this. However, one of my friends did say that in the middle of a conversation with the Ambassador's wife, she cut her off mid-sentence because she had 'seen someone more interesting to talk to!'

Feeling invisible or inadequate is not unusual for me as a diplomatic spouse, particularly given my ethnicity. For example, in Jakarta some people assumed I was a local. I organised a visit to a Kampung, a traditional village, for spouses to see how underprivileged people lived and to encourage volunteering there. I had never seen a Kampung before I started volunteering and I was particularly offended when someone said she thought I was raised in a Kampung, and was rather surprised that I had not been to one. It saddens me to think that people make those type of assumptions, and that my life revolves around my diplomat. Usually, I grin and bear it and rant privately to my diplomat, family and close friends back home. I then choose not to socialise with those people again. Eventually, I find a group of like-minded friends. In fact, I have been inspired and encouraged by many highly capable, high-achieving diplomatic spouses who have shared their experiences and their wisdom with me and who are interested in my life experience, too. Through these wonderful people, I have learned about the politics, education, healthcare and life in places like Hungary, Mexico, Switzerland, South Korea, Turkey, Tunisia, Colombia, Slovakia and Iran, but, most importantly, I have learned about them as individuals, too. Seeing the world through their eyes enriches my life and broadens my thinking. We spouses are people of the world, and I would argue with anyone who does not agree. It is a shame that often on posting we become invisible, labelled as 'only spouses', when we have so much to offer.

It is very frustrating to have to prove yourself each time you move, but these days, with experience and hindsight, I am not as bothered by my invisibility.

I did have the opportunity once to ask someone who has a great career of her own and whose spouse, a prominent politician and big personality, is always in the media, how she managed to keep her identity and how she felt when people were only interested in her spouse. Her advice was very good: 'Don't worry about what other people think'. It was like a light bulb switched on. She is right. I cannot make anyone be interested in me, and what they may think of me is actually not that important.

Keeping My Identity Through Volunteering

I have found that volunteering while at post provides me with a raison d'être and a connection to the community. It is also a good way to keep learning and up to date with changes in technology. When I went back to work in Australia after three years in Jakarta, technology had changed, and I felt truly inadequate. Who would have thought that you could print, fax, scan and photocopy all from one machine?

In Indonesia, I volunteered as a pre-school teacher for a charity in West Jakarta called Kampung Kids that provided a daily hot meal and pre-school for children whose parents could not afford it otherwise. The charity grew and added English and computer classes, and a sponsorship programme through which donors can sponsor a child's education in the hope that they can gain decent employment or even go on to university. It was such a joy to see the children I taught grow in confidence, learn and finally go to school. The gratitude from the children and their parents was so rewarding.

Volunteering turned out to be a good way to keep my brain active, retain my skills and reinvent myself. It has allowed me to do things I once loved but stopped doing as I moved up the corporate ladder. For example, I used to work in human resources in the learning and development field, and I loved developing and facilitating workshops; in my current post I am a training facilitator, running employability and communication workshops for the organisation's staff, volunteers and clients. I have been able to help spouses with their CVs so they can get jobs while they are at post; just about all the people I have helped have found work. It has been a good learning experience for me as well – it is fun to have conversations with spouses who are still learning English, and I have learned that there are words in English that do not translate so easily into other languages. I have thought about making a career change when I go back home, and volunteering in my field of interest could help me to do that.

Through volunteering, I have met a diverse range of people, including those experiencing difficult life situations. It is a good reminder to be grateful for the life I have. As a volunteer, I have always found that I get back more than I give, and more than I ever expected. The trust and gratitude I have received is worth more to me than money. The people I have met through volunteering are kind, caring and devoted to what they do. It is the perfect way to meet people, use my brain, do something I love and give back to the community. I could work while at post, but in some countries, unless I worked at our embassy or at another diplomatic mission, I might need to relinquish my diplomatic status.

Taking the Good with the Bad
Accompanying my diplomat to an overseas posting has benefits that far out way the negatives, but there is one large negative that I have to address.

Living with the Threat of Terrorism
You can make yourself comfortable with life at post, find the right balance of job, family, and volunteering and have all the technology in place to remain connected to home, but while everything may appear normal, there are things that are not within your control.

I have experienced, first-hand, terrorism at its worst. Our apartment block in Jakarta was bombed when I was at home and my diplomat was at work. More recently, there was a terrorist attack just down the road from where we live in London, at a place where I hang out regularly and where we take visitors or new spouses. In fact, we were in the vicinity just hours before the attack. Everyone is affected, but each in a different way. Some friends went home for a while after the Jakarta bombing, but I chose to stay and take advantage of the counselling that was offered to us. Once the counsellors went back to Australia, I kept in touch via phone and email for a couple of months until I felt I did not need to keep it up. I was lucky to be able to access this service and, of course, I had my diplomat, friends and family to talk to. It took about three months to feel safe, but I did get over it. It is particularly difficult for family and friends back home to comprehend why we just did not pack up and come home after these events, especially when my spouse's son was visiting at the time. (When things settled down, we organised for him to go back.) When the news broke about the bombings, my children wanted me to come home, but I told them that I would not leave and that I was OK and getting support from a counsellor. I also told them that security for staff and their families was stepped up and the apartment block we were living in also increased their security arrangements. It was hard for them to understand my reluctance to leave Jakarta (as the bombing was not close) but as the months went by they, too, became more comfortable with my decision. Daily phone calls to them helped and seeing armed police and military at shopping malls, airports and apartment blocks became the norm.

Social media means that the news is instantly spread all over the world, and as we know, sometimes what is reported is incorrect. During these crises, I made sure that I responded instantly to messages from home, so people knew that we were okay. I am really glad that I had discussed with my diplomat what to do in an emergency, where to go, where to meet if that is possible, and who to contact in London if he is not in the country. It has become a habit, since the bombings in Jakarta, that I let my diplomat know my movements – when I am leaving the house, where I am going, who I am meeting with and when I expect to be home. Once I am home, I let him know. If something were to happen, my diplomat would know whether I am in the affected area. He works long hours when a disaster happens, and it is likely that I may not see him for days. He always makes sure that he contacts me regularly, so he knows I am okay and that I know he is, too.

I do not dwell on the possibility of terrorism, though, nor do I feel afraid to go out or to travel. That would mean that those responsible would win. I am not saying that it has not affected me. Of course, it has. As I mentioned earlier, I sought counselling after the bombing in Jakarta and made sure that my spouse and others at post were supported, too. It took me many months to enjoy fireworks and not to recoil every time I heard sudden loud noises, like a door slamming or a balloon bursting.

Even though I am not afraid to go out on my own or travel, my experience has made me more aware of my surroundings. I trust my gut instinct if I find myself in a place where I feel uncomfortable, especially when I am on my own, but also when I am with friends or my spouse. An example of this is when leaving the theatre in London; we will leave quickly and not linger in the busy foyer after a show, because terrorists take advantage of crowded places for maximum damage. Making these kinds of decisions based on risk is a sad reality, not just for me but for everyone.

A Good Life

Even with such threats, the diplomatic life is positive in so many ways there is not space here to name them.

The wonderful, shared experiences in a different country; the opportunity to travel in our host country as well as other countries, and the support we give each other when times are tough have made us closer. Going on postings together is a unique life that can make or break relationships, and it has strengthened our bond as a couple. We have found ways to cope with stress, such as sharing our stories and, in time, turning potential nightmares into funny anecdotes. It is good to know that I have someone I trust and can rely on when I am so far away from my support network at home.

Diplomatic life has also provided me with more self-confidence, and while I struggle at times with feeling invisible, there is always something I can do about it. Talking to other spouses and sharing our experiences of what worked for them, and adapting their ideas to what works for me is great. It exposes me to new friendships, to other cultures, to learning about individuals and their personal experiences in ways I could never have done if I did not travel with my diplomat. I have found that I have so much life experience that I can share, too, that may be helpful to others.

For me, the chance to step in and out of my public service job, spend quality time with family and old friends, as well as to make these new friends at our embassy or from other countries, has been a joy and a privilege. I have discovered that I am much more than my career, and that happiness lies in my other roles, like being a grandmother. I have found pleasure in simple things like cooking. While most of the time I do not have to go anywhere if I do not want to, I realise that it is okay to stay at home all day if that is what I feel like doing. I have learned that I can have a positive impact wherever I end up, too.

The good times, when I cannot believe this is actually my life, occur far more often than the times when I feel lonely and isolated. I am very privileged to be a diplomat's spouse. I love my life and I love the fact that I am in a position in which I can give back to the community through my volunteering efforts. To me, it is like paying back the universe for all the wonderful experiences I have been lucky to have because I am a diplomat's spouse.

Our African Grey enjoying the Embassy swimming pool in Luanda

13 Foreign-born Diplomatic Spouses: Expect All of the Perks but More of the Stress

Carmen Davies

After 34 years as a foreign-born diplomatic spouse – that is, one not born in the country their spouse or partner[5] represents – I want to give readers, especially those considering becoming diplomatic spouses or who are already diplomatic spouses, advice on how to have an enjoyable life on postings and information about the kinds of stress they can expect. I collected these ideas from other spouses, from articles published in our diplomatic families' magazine, from interviews with spouses, and from lessons learned, at times the hard way, from 16 years of living overseas and 18 years of living in the UK.

In 1968, at the age of 21, I was a university student in Mexico City, the middle child of seven and the first to marry. I had met a British diplomat at a party, and soon after we became engaged. We were due to leave Mexico after our wedding since his temporary work assignment in the country capital was concluding, but, following the illness of an embassy colleague, we were asked whether we wanted to stay for a full term. We accepted gladly, and so I became the Mexican-born spouse of a British diplomat, and we ended up staying in Mexico for four years.

More Preparation and Language Work than Other Spouses
Fortunately for me, I began my new life near the people who had always helped me through difficult times. While I was learning the responsibilities of being married to a diplomat, I had a buffer from the realities of moving countries, living away from family and friends, and learning the language

---

5. Spouse/partner. Today many diplomatic couples, like others, are not spouses but unmarried long-term partners. In this article 'spouse' can be taken to mean 'spouse or partner', to avoid the need to repeat both words every time.

of the post country. Those challenges would come later, but any diplomatic spouse must be able to live happily with these, in addition to being interested in meeting new people and able to make new friends easily, to learn languages quickly, and to stay alone in a new country if their spouse has to travel as part of the job. We must all accept the restrictions that come along with our privileges, too; for example, we may be forbidden to work and earn a salary, or we may be required to host important events. It is not for everybody.

Foreign-born spouses must deal with another layer of difficulties on top of all of that. You will need to learn to speak and write (if not fluently, then to a good standard) the language of your spouse, and to learn as much as possible about the past and modern history, the customs, habits and political structure of your spouse's home country. It can be very useful, though it is not always possible, for a foreign-born spouse to spend some time in the diplomat's home country, becoming familiar with the life and language there before the couple goes on their first posting together.

You and your spouse both need to learn the language of the country you have been posted to as well. Even if you feel you will never be fluent, you need to learn as much as possible, if only so that you are prepared to deal with an emergency.

On the day our first child was due, and with my husband's grandmother (who spoke no Spanish) visiting Mexico for the birth of her great-grandchild, my husband suddenly became seriously ill with appendicitis. The solution turned out to be having my baby induced at the same hospital where my husband had his operation, while our staff at home made sure his grandmother was comfortable. I had a healthy boy, but my husband had complications and was so seriously ill that, as I learned later, the embassy had started making funeral plans. Without my family to help with baby care while my husband had two further operations, the six weeks he spent in the hospital, the most stressful time of my life, would have been even more difficult. I went into our first posting knowing that, as bad as that incident had been, the outcome might have been different if I had been in a strange country using a new language.

In fact, at our first posting in Africa, knowing the language may have saved our lives! Both of us had taken language courses, but we never imagined how soon after we arrived we would need them.

Our sixteen-year-old son had just flown in from London to spend his first holidays from boarding school with us in Angola. In the middle of the night, I woke to a banging noise, so loud I could hear it over our noisy air conditioning unit. I woke my husband. It was obvious somebody was in the garden or on the ground floor.

We switched the lights on and cautiously went downstairs, but everything seemed as normal, so we went back to the bedroom. As soon as we switched the lights off, the noise started up again. I ran to wake up our son and asked him to come to our balcony and tell me if he could see anything. Both my husband and I are short sighted, but our son had good vision. He saw two men in the garden hiding behind some bushes! I immediately shouted *'Gatuno! Gatuno! Policia! Policia!'* ('Thieves! Thieves! Police! Police!') at the top of my voice. Our next-door neighbour, a military man, came out onto his balcony with a gun and fired into the sky – and the intruders ran away. The loud noise I had heard was the two men snapping the bars that protected the house from the garden. They had been minutes away from breaking the grille on the door to the main entrance!

Our poor son thought his mother had gone crazy when I started to shout but I had never felt so happy to have learned the right words during our Portuguese language courses.

First Posting
To make a success of living overseas takes a lot of effort and ingenuity, but hundreds of spouses (not just foreign-born ones) manage this every day, and support is there if you know where to look. If you are lucky, as we were, some branch of your foreign service will provide a thorough, systematic pre-departure briefing about the situation in the destination country to eliminate some of the surprises and cushion some of the initial shocks. The UK's Foreign, Commonwealth and Development Office (FCDO) sponsors our Diplomatic Service Families Association (DSFA), which has provided UK- and foreign-born spouses with lots of information and support since its founding over 63 years ago.

Unfortunately, not all countries offer this kind of organisation. If yours is one that does not, you can take the initiative. My advice to you, and to all diplomatic spouses, is to begin on day one. Do not delay or postpone. Meet other spouses or meet some locals, explore your city, look for work or for a volunteer position, but do something, and start at once. You will not necessarily find exactly the thing you want to do at first, but if you do something, then you will put yourself into an active mode and the rest will follow – and you will learn some of the things your foreign service might not have briefed you on.

If you cannot find a job (or spouses are not permitted to work in your post country), look for a place to volunteer – you will find opportunities to help with charities, schools and orphanages. If you do not find a place to work, come up with your own project: in Zagreb, in 1981, the wife of a businessman and I created a monthly newsletter in English for the foreign community. We organised monthly trips for the spouses of diplomats and foreign businesspeople to Trieste and Graz, and to do some shopping. We kept ourselves very active, enjoying living in what was at the time one of the most open communist countries. You could try something similar, promoting to other foreign residents the unusual places that you have discovered in your new country.

Making friends with local people will be easier if you have small children since you can meet other parents, but you can make friends where you work or volunteer, too. You will find this easier, and be less likely to offend others, if you do not make yourself sound unpleasant; at social gatherings, try not to complain or grumble about the new place. Many times, at our first posting in Mexico City, I heard wives complaining about silly things or making remarks about Mexico, which were not pleasant to hear. Some spouses never bothered to learn the language, too, and when they went to do their shopping, just pointed to what they wanted and signalled the amounts with their fingers.

Emotional Strains on Diplomatic Spouses, UK and Foreign-born
All diplomatic spouses will have vivid memories of their first postings, including the difficulties in adjusting to their new lives, but foreign-born spouses may suffer extra anxieties. Just think about questions of etiquette: you will need to know the rules of social behaviour for your diplomatic spouse's home country as well as the customs of the Diplomatic Service itself. For me, entertaining at our first post not only involved lots of time in planning, researching what food was available and preparing it, but also involved being always afraid of offending by saying or doing the wrong thing in front of colleagues and guests, even though our first Head of Mission and his wife were very nice.

Whether you are a foreign-born spouse or were born to your diplomat spouse's nationality, whether female or male, being married to a diplomat will probably make you feel, sooner or later, like an unofficial employee of the service. This is not necessarily a bad thing; if you help your spouse you have the satisfaction of being a part of your spouse's good results, which some find a satisfying career in itself. The higher the diplomat's rank, the more demands may fall on the spouse. You may be called on not only for entertaining or dealing with embassy staff, but for sorting out all kinds of problems that a spouse outside the diplomatic world might never have to deal with: the need to help the families or the house staff of members of the mission after serious illnesses, accidents, or even bereavements, or a sudden need to take guests into your home after some traumatic incident involving fellow nationals.

The stresses of leaving family behind when you move to a posting might include leaving your children back in your home country; the UK Diplomatic Service families I knew spoke often of unhappiness and guilt about leaving children at boarding schools. News from your children or their schools may at times be disturbing, leaving you feeling impotent, distressed by your inability to step in right away. The trials of adolescence, such as when a child leaves school, may call for more parental guidance, too.

Having friends who understand your social situation can help. My advice is not to fall into the trap of deciding not to make close friendships in order to spare yourself painful separations but to take advantage of whatever opportunities for friendship you have, especially since these may be somewhat limited. When we were in Zagreb, the mission was very small, but that was only one of the limitations. I knew several spouses then, of both British diplomats and businessmen, who only spoke English, and the language barrier was high at the time; if you only spoke English, your world, and the range of available contacts, could be very narrow.

On postings in developed countries, the problem here is that there is often no organised or cohesive expatriate or diplomatic community, and people just get left to make their own way. In 'difficult' countries, by contrast, the expat community tends to stick together more and provide a supporting network. Lack of mobility due to societal restrictions on women can also cause loneliness and minimise contact with the country and culture outside. Spouses who get lonely and depressed generally do not confide in others, so staying connected is important.

Unfortunately, struggling because of mental stress is often still not understood or considered acceptable, so opening up about the problem of stress within the mission may not be safe or advisable in case it could harm your spouse's standing and career. Also, you will probably be expected to support your diplomat if there are problems at the office, perhaps by listening to grievances, even when sometimes your diplomat is unable to do the same in return – whether that is due to workload, a lack of understanding, or simply being personally unequipped emotionally to offer what a stressed spouse needs. Other spouses may not be responsive or able to do anything for a spouse in trouble in some cases: where there are signs of drinking too much or of marriage difficulties, intervention is often considered inappropriate.

If a marriage ends in separation or divorce, a diplomatic spouse will be in an even weaker position than most ex-spouses in finding a job, due to relocations and restrictions on working that can leave a diplomatic spouse with a patchy work history, or none at all. Having been out of employment can also lead to a reduced pension, though some foreign services do offer help; the British FCDO, for example, now offers spouses pension compensation from the very first post, but other countries may not do the same. After even a short period, some professionals will not only have gaps in their CVs but may find that their qualifications are out of date. They may need to retrain or change to a different line of work. If your diplomat spouse's employer offers any help towards retraining, as ours does (via the DSFA), you might need to arrange that before you sever ties entirely. (A foreign-born spouse might have further difficulties because of not having qualifications that are accredited in the UK.)

More serious and long-lasting effects of the stress of living as a diplomatic spouse need to be acknowledged as well. Being a member of a diplomatic community provides a privileged way of life but also an artificial one, and some people adapt better than others; family separations and splits, disjointed education, and a sense of rootlessness can result in symptoms ranging from simple unhappiness or loneliness, through bitterness or despair, all the way to broken marriages, alcoholism or psychological disturbance. You may find that having to move on again after settling in a posting can be very distressing: leaving the house when you have only recently furnished and organised it; leaving friends that it took so much effort to make; leaping again into the unknown. You may feel like you are constantly making and then breaking relationships, and that everyone just expects you to be able to cope. Seeking help is still often perceived as a sign of weakness and failure, although this, fortunately, has been improving, and there is help available nowadays. This is one of the areas where the UK's DSFA has been of tremendous service.

Emotional Strains on Spouses Returning 'Home'
On your posting, you may have worked closely with your diplomat spouse and contributed to the representational work of the mission. Once home, you become a private individual again, the representational element becomes remote, and you will need to adjust to a new identity. Just as on a posting, days can be very long in a new environment before you establish or re-establish relationships. You may run into serious obstacles that prevent you from accomplishing all that you had hoped to achieve. Even though you are at home, you will run into some of the same difficulties you found on your post, such as getting things unpacked and setting up all your computer/electrical gadgets. Your diplomat spouse's long and irregular hours may prevent you from making regular commitments by way of getting a job or enrolling for serious hobbies or classes, especially if you have small children at home.

When we moved from Mexico to London, which would become our home base, we all had to adjust. My husband had to adapt to a new position and to commuting. He left at 8.30 a.m. and came home at 7.00 p.m., leaving me to unpack, organise the home, take care of our son, cook, clean, everything. None of his family or friends lived near us. I wanted to work but I could not (and voluntary work, while rewarding, would have demanded time, effort and a similar commitment). Our priorities were to find a place to live and a school for our two-year-old son. Eventually, he would go to a nursery, but he did not go immediately. There were not enough places, so we could not get him in. There was no way that I could have left my son, who was also returning to live in London for the first time; people forget that even small children have needs when adapting to a new country. I only got a job when my son was just over four years old, and we employed an au pair who lived with us.

Can you imagine families having to leave pets behind? We had to leave our parrot, who lived with us for 20 years, when we left our last posting. In 1988, we received Santos, an African Grey parrot, as a present in Angola. He came back to England with us, and then went out again to Namibia, back to

England, and finally to Panama. We thought it would be better for him to stay in Panama, where the weather is tropical and he could live outdoors, instead of returning with us to live indoors in colder London. Santos was bilingual, speaking both Spanish and English. He did funny things. When he wanted to go to sleep, he would screech and say 'Goodnight' until we covered his cage and turned the lights off. He was such a character! We left Santos with the family of a member of the Residence's staff who lived in the countryside, so he could live in a larger space in the tropical environment that he was born to. Parrots can live up to 50 or 60 years.

Even those without the complication of pets will have a lot of adjusting to do, sometimes in ways you may never have thought of. Coming home, for example, might mean adapting social activities to a different climate. You may have exchanged a large house in a good residential area for an inner-city environment; alternatively, if you find yourself living outside the home capital, you may miss the lively capital-city experience of your posting. You could even find yourself having to come to terms with living with peace and plenty, as I did when I returned home after three years in Angola, a hardship posting. Due to a civil war and a curfew every night, supplies of food and goods in general were difficult to come by. Shopping in London again, I found myself uncomfortable at times, walking into a supermarket and seeing rows and rows of articles of the same kind – an aisle of different detergents, say – and having to choose one item! It took months for me to re-adapt to all the choices of provisions that we enjoy in the UK.

The Foreign-born Spouse of a Head of Mission

In my time, expectations regarding the supporting role of a diplomatic spouse, especially the spouse of a Head of Mission, were still quite high. At least in the British Diplomatic Service they are nowadays much more relaxed, even officially non-existent.

All the same, the appointment of a diplomat to be Head of Mission can raise the pressure on the diplomat's spouse, too, especially if they are posted to one of the more globally important countries. The Residence may become a hotel for a succession of prominent visitors; the spouse can feel always on parade – moving in the most distinguished company and receiving almost royal treatment at times, though relationships may only be superficial. I met people from all over the world when I was the spouse of the Head of Mission – VIPs, distinguished visitors from my husband's country, including Lady

Thatcher some years after she left office, and leading local personalities — and I contributed to special events, such as the installation of a bronze bust of Dame Margot Fonteyn, the ballerina, at the Teatro Nacional in Panama.

While this role has its glamorous side, some may feel it as an enormous burden, one that cannot always be shared with other spouses at the mission. You meet and host people, but you may never see them again, and you live in a fishbowl: everybody watches you all the time. Also, the Head of Mission and his/her spouse have a crucial effect, for good or ill, on the happiness and mental health of those under them in the hierarchy. How determined you may be not to be seduced by the glamour; it can go to your head. Developing close friendships with spouses of the Heads of Missions from friendly countries may only distance you further from the other spouses of your own mission and make relationships with them more formal.

Foreign-born spouses of Heads of Mission feel these problems more acutely. Many foreign-born wives or husbands overplay their role by becoming more identified with their spouse's country, denying their own national identity, or else they withdraw from identification with their spouse's country and over-assert their original national identity, creating additional hurdles to surmount. At times, it is hard to maintain your own identity as an individual while responding to the demands of a role that requires you to be someone quite different.

In my own case, we were very lucky in our postings, and my being from Mexico became an asset to my husband. Many good relationships were made in various countries due to my being a foreign-born spouse; at all our postings, being married to a Latin woman meant he was perceived as easier to get along with.

The Negative and the Positive
There is no doubt that Diplomatic Service spouses have to make more sacrifices than spouses of people in other professions. Not only do they suffer the very great inconvenience of frequent moves from one country to another, with the consequent damaging effects on their own qualifications or their own job opportunities, but they may feel obliged to put a great deal more time and effort into supporting their spouse in this particular profession. Foreign-born spouses may find their duties weigh even more heavily, and they may suffer more stress.

On the other hand, to be a diplomatic spouse is a deeply rewarding role. I have been extremely privileged to have lived in so many countries and to have met many wonderful people. I have also been honoured to have been shown places not often open to the public, such as the old diamond area between Lüderitz and Oranjemund in Namibia and the private island research station of the Smithsonian Institute in Panama.

Back at our home base in London, I still have a life full of interest, variety and challenge with an enlarging circle of friends in the Diplomatic Spouses Club of London, in our DSFA at the Foreign Office and in the Foreign and Commonwealth Office Association (FCOA), the serving and retired diplomats' association. I feel extremely proud of the support provided by our DSFA, especially since I can see how the spouses of some foreign diplomats struggle because their countries do not have the equivalent. I will always thank the Foreign Office for providing me with one of the most important tools: learning the languages of the countries where we were posted.

Living overseas, and in so many different environments, you become less insular than people who have spent their whole lives in one country; you gain an invaluable understanding of how the rest of the world actually operates. While living abroad can also give you the experience of being the odd one out, it is good for us all to be put into a position where we can begin to appreciate how immigrants might feel. We, the foreign-born spouses, by leaving our own nations, learning other languages and living in several countries, become members of the international community – belonging not to one country but to many – and through this, we have become truly globalised!

The secret is to learn how to adopt the challenges we face.

(Aila Images/shutterstock.com)

14 The Journey Towards Establishing a Diplomatic Spouse Club

Agnes Fenyvesy

I am the wife of a Hungarian diplomat, previously posted in London. I hold a master's degree in Public Administration and work as a senior civil servant when on a home posting. I was born into a non-diplomatic family. My mother was a judge for decades. We moved to a new house regularly, so I was used to changing residences.

I became a diplomatic spouse at a relatively early stage when I met my future husband at the age of eighteen. Shortly after we met, he was posted to Asia and, at the same time, I moved to the US, which made our lives complicated. Deepening my relationship with my diplomat was the best decision of my life, but it made my journey a bit bumpy.

My husband's first posting was a hardship posting, so I did not think about moving there permanently. I only visited him several times for long periods while I was focusing on my own studies back home.

The years passed quickly, and I enjoyed all the excitement of travelling to the exotic east, which I knew only from books and TV. I made true and long-lasting friendships, learned the recipes of hundreds of delicious dishes and explored the neighbourhood as much as we were allowed to, but I had less chance to learn the local language, except for a few words. This posting was a very pleasant time for me. I enjoyed all the benefits while not having the proper responsibilities of a diplomatic spouse. This life suited me at that time. I had an extremely good relationship with the embassy staff, but it was a small mission. I received hundreds of invitations when visiting there, though, and also had plenty of time for myself.

This posting influenced my life very much, including my studies and, based on the experiences gained there, I finished my dissertation dedicated to the conflict in Afghanistan. This really established my never-ending interest in that region.

In spite of this comfortable, occasionally visiting lifestyle, I wanted to become a real accompanying diplomatic partner. That time came after my graduations and work experience, almost a decade later, when we were posted to London. I was extremely excited at becoming a real diplomatic wife – a dream come true!

I remembered committing all the protocol mistakes it is possible to make during the Asia posting, particularly at the first seated dinner reception I attended, so I dug into etiquette books, which are vital in our life. I still need to use them many times and would recommend them for everyone to understand correct behaviour.

I imagined myself attending fancy receptions at different embassies. I dreamt about fulfilling my duties as a diplomatic wife: hosting events in our home; participating in many interesting conversations on different topics; being involved in organisational work; seeing lots of other diplomats and their partners; meeting with local politicians, professors, civil servants and having a wide social life. I felt important, in a way. I even found suitable outfits for a huge variety of events, including meeting the Queen and the Royal Family. Well, I was privileged enough to meeting Her Majesty, but it was not exactly as I imagined earlier.

Reality set in when we arrived in our new destination and moved into our flat. Unfortunately, there were financial cuts everywhere, including to embassy budgets and spouses were hardly invited to events. The embassy staff were busy with work and not with welcoming new colleagues and their families. We only had three families; the rest of the staff was single. There were associations for diplomats but not for their partners. The only option was the Young Diplomats in London (YDL), a voluntary organisation that provides a forum for diplomats in London to network, occasionally welcoming the partners at their activities. So, I soon faced a less optimistic reality compared to my dreams.

To avoid any misunderstandings, I do not mean to complain. It is just a fact that the start to our life in London was not easy.

It is usually believed that diplomatic families have a fairy tale life. Wives do not need to have a job, only being housewives who attend fancy receptions, where they dress up in the latest fashions and chat while drinking expensive champagne. I have heard diplomatic spouses defined as 'Ferrero Rocher Princesses', which I object to.

So, our London posting was completely different to the life we had before, and also to the life I imagined.

I had to get used to the fact that my husband arrived home late due to the amount of work he needed to finish in a day, or attending those receptions I wished to attend but had not received an invitation to. I had to get used to being alone and dealing with our new life, learning the cultural differences, establishing new relationships, doing the heavy shopping by myself with my trolley bag, accepting the different quality of ingredients and taste of food, and gaining the understanding of different local habits.

The period of time it takes to settle down in a post differs city by city, person by person. I have an extroverted personality, but even I had difficulties with it. I wished I had had more support. Then, I settled down both physically and mentally, and started to focus on myself and what to do with my spare time.

I realised this was a real opportunity to do what I wanted to do and tried to enjoy my new environment as much as possible. London is one of the best places on Earth, but also frightening at the beginning.

I attended a language course just to be amongst others to talk to during the day. I had no job at the embassy and had tried to be an apprentice elsewhere, but faced closed doors all the time due to my diplomatic status.

In my opinion, being a diplomatic wife is quite challenging. Yes, our lifestyle is appealing for those who have never tried it. I was extremely excited when I met my husband, thinking that we would travel the world, meet interesting people and have a privileged life. Actually, I have done all these things. I feel glad to be part of the foreign service, but it is not that girly dream come true.

It is a difficult job to be nice all the time, being an excellent host, constantly supporting your other half, taking care of the whole family, being up to date with the latest news, trying not to hurt others while representing the interests of your own country and to look good even when you shop at the local market. Doing all of these while you are in a foreign country, in a strange environment with a different culture, while being far away from home and from your normal life is not easy.

How to 'treat' diplomatic spouses has always been a sensitive question. Fifty years ago, wives were not allowed to work while at post. Now, it is more widely accepted, although it depends on local regulations. Sometimes, the home country has strict regulations against it. In theory, you can work in a foreign country, in reality it is not easy at all. Even if you are lucky enough with the rules, it is the local job market that makes it more difficult. Employers avoid hiring staff with diplomatic status.

The status of diplomatic spouses and families has been an ever-present question in the history of diplomacy. Recently, this has received more attention. For example, EUFASA, the European Union Foreign Affairs Spouses Association, was founded to support the families of diplomats in the European Union countries, focusing on different fields, such as legal status, employment, education, etcetera. It was a wife of a diplomat who came up with the idea of meeting amongst the different European Ministries of Foreign Affairs' spouses associations. For many years, wives fought for their rights; for their voices to be heard; for representation. I have maintained a good relationship with the participants I met at the EUFASA London Conference in 2019, which was hosted by the Foreign, Commonwealth and Development Office's Diplomatic Service Families Association (DSFA).

Nowadays, the question is: do we need this kind of association? In my opinion, yes, it is vital, but not all spouses agree with me. Even my own national association has recently brought the curtain down.

We are all different. We all have different backgrounds, experiences and needs when we go to a post abroad. Some might need a little help settling down in a new environment, some prefer to do it alone. Some countries provide enough help for their staff overseas, some not. What connects us is the constant change in our lives from country to country representing our homeland. Wherever life takes us, we serve our country.

Diplomatic spouses are usually divided into two groups, those who wish to be involved in the traditional duties of a diplomat's partner, and those who do not. Personally, I belong to the first group, but many of my friends belong to the second.

It depends on the personality, the seniority, the destination and the situation you are in which path you follow during your post. I discussed this with my friends, and we did not all agree. Some agree that this is not only the diplomat's job, but we also have responsibilities while being abroad with them. There is an increasing number in the diplomatic community who claim it is only the other halves who have the diplomatic job; the partners should not take part in it. Obviously, there are cases we cannot be involved in, but in everyday life there are many times when the diplomat in the family needs our help.

I had a tough conversation with one of my fellows, who supports the opposition. She does not like being involved in anything when they are abroad, does not like attending any events and does not belong to any association supporting diplomatic families. I understand this point of view, but I disagree.

I believe in the power of belonging to a community, in our case belonging to the diplomatic spouses' community. It can help you to settle down smoothly, to meet true friends, to explore the posting destination with other spouses from all over the world and to find your way to reinvent yourself again and again.

I think the secret is to learn how to enjoy all kinds of environment and different people, and how to adopt the challenges we face to our own life. The post could be the best place on the planet, but you will not enjoy it if you are not open to the world. To be a diplomatic spouse, it is necessary to be extroverted, friendly, educated and open-minded. We should see and recognise the smallest things that bring a smile and makes us happy. Believe me, many people do not realise how lucky they are.

In my opinion, diplomatic spouses do not receive enough attention, despite all the efforts of local and international associations. This is for many reasons, but one of them might be the fact that the new generation of diplomatic spouses do not wish to be part of this exciting, yet challenging lifestyle. Many decide not to accompany their partners abroad. Rather, they focus on their own career, which can hardly be successful when moving every four years in order to keep the family together.

On the other hand, spouses who sacrifice themselves to fulfil their diplomat partner's duties are almost invisible to those outside. Based on my experiences, the general attitude towards us shows a lack of understanding. Governments do not always compensate for losing our jobs just to accompany our other halves abroad, not to mention the pension systems we are cut out of. People not being involved in the foreign service cannot understand our feelings as we follow our families all around the globe, while losing our roots back home. We are 'home' at all our destinations, but always temporarily. We widen our knowledge and experience of all the countries we live in, while missing being close to our loved ones at home.

Being a diplomatic spouse is complicated and this life does not suit all of us. It is necessary to understand all the implications of this lifestyle when falling in love with a diplomat.

Early in the history of diplomacy, diplomatic spouses were trained for this life, as it was the privilege of the upper class. Ladies were able to deal with organising the whole household, keeping everything in order even in extreme circumstances, and were keen on delivering their best while at post. They were involved in the life of the embassies, were responsible for each other abroad, met regularly and tried to help where it was needed. They felt that they were also representing their country abroad and were keen on giving something back to the host state through voluntary work. This norm has changed over time, dramatically so in the last decade.

The chance and the opportunity of being a diplomat has risen significantly, while the selection for this job has changed considerably. Spouses usually do not receive special guidance in preparation for the posting anymore, but might receive a short training before starting their new life abroad. This is not necessarily enough to understand all the nuances of the expectations towards us. I see there are fields where progress is needed.

I remember one of my most embarrassing moments. At a reception I was asked about my opinion on a case, which challenged the government I represented. There are many communication skills which should be taught to us as well, not just to the diplomats. Luckily, I was prepared for this kind of question.

I also see that there are many highly qualified spouses who struggle to find opportunities to share their knowledge for the benefit of the hosting country. I think distribution of the enormous knowledge we all bring into a destination could be improved.

I believe this is a beautiful life, but sometimes spouses need more attention, and our voices should be heard on issues regarding our circumstances. So, I was keen on joining a spouses' club in London, but because I could not find one, I created one, called the Diplomatic Spouses Club in London (DSCL).

DSCL

The lack of invitations to accompany my husband to diplomatic events in London meant that there were few opportunities to meet other spouses. I desperately wanted to feel that I belonged somewhere (beside to my beloved hubby), where people could understand me and value my efforts as a diplomatic wife.

I wished to join a diplomatic group where I could volunteer, or at least to attend some activities, but my search was not successful. The only group dedicated to diplomatic families was the DSFA, but this organisation was for the families of British diplomats.

Finally, I came up with the idea of establishing the missing association in London's diplomatic life and founded DSCL, The Diplomatic Spouses Club in London, which opened its doors to the spouses of diplomats, regardless of seniority, posted in London from all over the globe.

I wanted to create a friendly, informal, welcoming atmosphere where the spouses could meet up, share information and get to know each other, while enjoying social and cultural life together and exploring what London and the UK could offer.

I believed that there were many spouses who needed a welcoming group to meet. I started DSCL in an informal way by inviting those I had met for short visits to discover London, and organised low-budget events, as we had no financial support at all. Then, from the wives of heads of missions, I received highly appreciated help to spread the word, particularly from the doyenne of the Diplomatic Corps in London, Mrs Dalal Al-Duwaisan, the wife of the Kuwaiti Ambassador, who was keen on this project and welcomed my ideas. Similarly, Ms Elizabeth Stewart, the editor of the *Embassy* magazine, who has encouraged me since we met and was so generous to give me the platform at the Embassy Induction Seminars to share my views. Then, I met a lovely British diplomatic spouse who became my greatest support to get the essential connections in London. Let me take this opportunity to express my gratitude to Mrs Carmen Davies (and also to Mr Davies) for all her never-ending efforts through the years for DSCL. Without her, I would not have been able to achieve my goals.

The beginning was not easy at all, as I had to share my time between London and Budapest due to my parents' health problems, but I remember perfectly the very first official DSCL event. It was a piano concert at the Hungarian Cultural Centre, given by a talented Japanese pianist, Ms Masako Kamikawa, who lives in Germany, but practices in London. This event's success gave me stamina to continue this project.

Then, I realised that with the number of members gained, we needed to structure the association.

Months of organisational works followed, which were probably invisible for most of the members, but I really enjoyed meeting all the helpful people I contacted about the new association: lawyers, accountants, journalists, diplomats, other leaders of associations, professors, company directors for sponsorship and British diplomatic partners. I also paid a visit to the DFSA for advice and future collaboration, beginning our good relationship, which by now is stronger than ever, and to YDL, the Young Diplomats in London (young means young spirit). The YDL presidents at that time welcomed my ideas and helped to organise joint events. They also invited our members to their events.

Soon, this small, friendly group of people became a proper diplomatic association, valued in London's diplomatic life. It is led by a President and run by a committee board, with about a hundred members. A small membership fee is collected to maintain the association and it is based on a written Constitution. To complete this, it was quite useful that I had previous legal and financial studies and experience. Basically, I wrote the constitution for our club based on the rules of other diplomatic groups. I wanted to make the DSCL as democratic and as globally represented as possible. I investigated the financial regulations in the UK and whether any registration was needed for the club. I dealt with the everyday issues and the growing interest in different positions amongst the members, agreed on special offers for our members with the diplomatic supplier companies (Chacalli and IDS), accepted the offer of a business address from the Belize High Commissioner to start with and I jumped into the never-ending negotiations with Lloyds Bank to open an account for the association. I wanted the club to be absolutely financially transparent. Opening a bank account took more than a year to complete, though.

Although the club is led by the president, all the decisions are made by the committee. This board is elected annually by the club's members at the Annual General Meeting. The candidates are volunteers. Sub-clubs, such as a kid's club or a book club, are created under the DSCL umbrella.

I was extremely happy to announce the establishment of our club officially and to start the everyday business with a group of volunteers from all around the globe. I send special thanks to all who helped me and offered their time for this project.

As the club started to grow, needs changed, and to help fulfil our duties, we received generous financial support from the Consular Corps, for which I thank them.

I was responsible for organising hundreds of activities for the club's members, including: piano concerts; visits to the Houses of Parliament, to the Supreme Court, to the Royal Courts of Justice and to the Bars; coffee mornings; museum and gallery tours; English lessons to improve our pronunciation and widen our vocabulary; family days for the diplomatic families, such as our most successful Egg Hunt, generously sponsored by Jaguar and Landrover; wine tasting; jewellery, fashion and colour shows; cultural events hosted by embassies for our members; seminar talks on different topics and, amongst many other events, International Women's Day celebrations with guest speakers and lectures provided by academies and universities for our members. I also managed to provide free foreign language courses for our members, based on an agreement with a university. At this point may I express my gratitude to all who were involved in organising events for DSCL.

To crown our activities, we met Ms Marina Wheeler, the wife of the British Foreign Secretary at that time (later the British Prime Minister, Boris

Johnson) through the Embassy of Hungary. I am extremely grateful for all the support I received from them while I organised DSCL, and to all the other embassies who hosted us.

During the years, I faced the challenges of being the leader of a big group. I learnt how to be diplomatic and tough at the same time; how to represent a group of people, especially towards the business sector; how to select committed people for board positions; how to allocate duties while keeping an eye on all the details; how to be responsible for my team, even if there are differences between us, and how to get others to be team players.

Some of these lessons I learnt the hard way. I remember my first business meeting, with a large, multi-national company, for example. It was an unexpected opportunity, and I had never attended such a session before, so I had no idea what to expect. We discussed the situation of DSCL and our needs, and how we could mutually help each other. This was at the very beginning of organising the DSCL. We only had our mailing list set up. There were no bank accounts, no records, no official board yet. It was as if the DSCL did not exist, and I felt intimidated when this was pointed out. It was a good lesson for me; I was much more prepared for my later business meetings.

I believe that, after all this excitement, the most difficult part is to leave everything behind.

I see that recently the structure and the constitution of DSCL has been changed for its members' current needs. Obviously DSCL has an ever-changing membership according to the constant location change of the diplomatic lifestyle. People come and go. They perhaps have different needs and expectations.

I know the DSCL is in good hands and has a very committed board to make it even better. I wish more people would become involved with it. I hope, too, that DSCL is strong enough to remain an individual association dedicated to the international diplomatic community posted in London and will serve their needs into the future. Many of the ladies and gentlemen who heard about my ideas became DSCL members. Being involved in this beautiful enterprise from the beginning was my pleasure and I wish longevity to this much-needed association. I look forward to witnessing its adulthood while watching it from a distance, now we have left London. I am really grateful for all of the opportunities I had, the knowledge I gained and for all the friends I met.

I understand that my ideas have inspired other groups. It makes me proud to see the increasing number of different diplomatic groups in London since I started DSCL. My input into its diplomatic platform is paying off and all my time spent in London and my efforts dedicated to the benefits of other diplomatic partners are recognized.

I hope I have illustrated that there is no good or bad posting destination. You should not judge it by the geographical situation. You always have opportunities to enjoy your life during your time there. You should never give up your ideas and do not give depression a chance, even if you face challenges at first. You really should look around, notice the cheerful things and follow your dreams, even if you have to create them yourself.

Despite the ups and downs of our lifestyle, I am happy to be a diplomatic spouse. I appreciate all I have learnt from diplomatic opportunities. I look forward to being involved in the diplomatic life in Washington DC, our new destination.

We live in real historical times and I am happy to witness these from the front row: the election resulted with Karzai's presidency during our first post, Brexit during our London time and now the Biden administration after the election of the century in the United States.

Photograph: Margarita Mavromichalis, www.margaritamavromichalis.com

15 Sketches of a Diplomat's Spouse on a Coronised Canvas

Zoofa Talha

Life of a Diplomat's Spouse: a Saga of Twists and Turns

> 'You have diplomatic immunity!'
> 'You enjoy a lavish lifestyle.'
> 'You are on an extended vacation.'
> 'You live a tax-free life!'
> 'You don't have to do anything because you have help.'
> 'You taste a variety of global cultures.'

These are a few of the statements I have heard as the wife of a diplomat over the last four years. Besides these exaggerated privileges, there is a rollercoaster of emotions and anxieties associated to this lifestyle.

My childhood dream was to be a medical practitioner. I was practicing as a dentist in my native country, Pakistan, when I married a diplomat. Our wedding did not bring about any major switch in my professional life and I continued working as before.

Six months later, we got the news of our first posting, to Argentina. I had no idea what it was going to be like. But I was sure about one thing, that I had to continue my career wherever we go.

Arriving in a land with a different language and culture, and altogether a different lifestyle, brought about struggles I had not realised were associated with being a diplomat's spouse. It began with discovering that no dentistry courses were offered in the English language in Buenos Aires and there was no diplomatic arrangement to allow me to work in the country. These realities stressed me. I had no previous knowledge of Spanish,

Argentina, or Latin America. I overcame such stresses by thinking about the fact that I would have more time to enjoy with my family. We were blessed with a baby boy during the first year of our posting. It was a life-changing and pleasing advancement in our lives.

It has been three years now. I am Dr. Zoofa, currently living in Argentina with my husband and a two-and-a-half-year-old son. My husband is a diplomat and is posted in Buenos Aires. I am a dentist professionally but not practicing here due to licensing issues and that is the only, but immense, imperfection in an otherwise perfect life here in Argentina.

Resilience Born of a Pandemic

Being the mother of a toddler is a nerve-racking experience and in a global pandemic, in a foreign land, alone, pregnancy can be even scarier. They say, "It's much easier the second time". But whosoever said that surely was not pregnant during a pandemic.

It was an incredibly happy start to November 2019 when we realised that we were going to have our second baby. My son was already going to a kindergarten and life was going exceptionally smoothly and pleasantly. Then, two months later, I started hearing the news of Coronavirus affecting China on a large scale. For me, it was just another piece of news that I come across daily. I had no idea that it was something that would reach my doorstep and turn my life upside down.

It was the start of March 2020 when Coronavirus appeared in Argentina and for me the world started changing then. Suddenly, everything landed on my shoulders. My son was not going to kindergarten anymore. Domestic assistance was no longer there. Markets and shopping places closed and the fear of the known but unseen virus was covering the landscape rapidly. Owing to its novel entity, healthcare professionals did not know much about it. So, putting pregnant women in the risk group added further anxiety and stress to my mind.

Every day was a challenge for me now. My doctor forbade me from coming to the hospital during the nationwide lockdown. Being away from parents, family and my entire support system was already disturbing in the pandemic situation and not going for the prenatal tests just added further gloominess to the circumstances. This whole episode was nothing like I had anticipated, ever. I stayed at home for two months, hoping only for the end of the pandemic before I delivered. After two months of sheer uncertainty, my doctor called me to the hospital in May 2020. Prenatal check-ups could not be delayed any further. Every time I went to the hospital, my son and husband waited outside as they were not allowed to accompany me. On one such visit, I was told that I would not be allowed to be escorted by my small family in Argentina during my labour. I had horrible nightmares for weeks thinking, *I am going to deliver my baby when I am all alone!* Every evening, I used to spend a great deal of time with my husband, trying to find answers to unanswerable questions. How to handle the upcoming situation? Will I be able to manage everything alone? How will my son get by without me? We ended up hoping that God would take us through it.

It was a freezing morning in July, before dawn, when I had to rush to the hospital leaving my son and husband behind. My son was sleeping when I said goodbye to both with a very heavy heart and tears in my eyes. Driving alone through the silent roads of Buenos Aires, quiet due to the longest lockdown in the world, I felt waves of despair inside me that were at the same frequency as the waves of desperation existing in the suffocating air of this city. On arrival at the hospital, when I needed support and someone on my side giving me courage, staff were sanitizing my hands, and asking me about my temperature and shortness of breath. Yes, I had shortness of breath but not from Corona, from my emotions and the contractions I was having! The situation at the hospital was challenging. My Spanish was not good, and the hospital staff knew only Spanish. The arrival of my doctor was the only ray of hope as she could communicate with me in English.

It was a baby girl, and I was happy to the core, but I was alone. No one was there to share my happiness. No one to take her from my arms with gratitude. And my lovely son was also away from me. I spent two days at hospital feeling happy and sad simultaneously. The experience of my first childbirth was wonderful. This second time was way more empowering and brought more resilience. It was a learning phase of my life, which taught me courage to face the hardest challenges of life in a powerful and resilient way. I hope to pass this strength and power to my daughter one day when I will tell her stories of her birth.

A practicing doctor and a medical instructor collapsed into a housewife in a foreign land, looking after a toddler without any domestic help and then giving birth amidst a pandemic situation are all phases of my life, during this one posting. These experiences have given more energy, positivity and light into my soul. And yes, this has also unveiled rough patterns of life with a diplomat, which are usually camouflaged and concealed.

Soul Searching in a Pandemic
I believe that our bodies are deeply connected with our souls. The soul also bears the consequences of the things that we embrace physically. The whole incidence of the birth of my daughter was accompanied by a cascade of emotions.

At the start of March 2020, when the corona episode started in Buenos Aires, it felt like clouds of gloominess covered the entire city. Closed restaurants and shopping malls, and empty roads, gave the impression of a venom circulating in the streets. The summer collapsing into autumn added despair to the situation.

I did not fully perceive the intensity of the issue in the beginning. For me, spending more time with the family, playing more with my son, cooking for hours, ordering stuff online and watching TV for the whole day were the positive aspects of the pandemic.

With every passing day, though, I started realizing that they were just temporary reliefs, and the coin had another side as well, which was more devastating than I had ever imagined.

I realized that change is a fundamental element of life.

I realized that my son was growing physically but mentally he was stuck between narrow boundaries.

I realized that the word 'tiredness' has many dimensions. It comes not only with hectic routine but with not doing enough as well.

I realized that nature was healing, but human life was degenerating.

I realized that beside the fear of being infected by the virus, additional problems came for me. Maintaining physical distance from my loved ones, being stranded in a foreign country and just the fact of being stuck at home were some major issues which I encountered.

Being the spouse of a diplomat is already an isolating and challenging experience sometimes. All magic comes with a price. The joys of roaming around the world and living in global capitals comes with the price of loss of identity and social isolation for diplomatic spouses. The 'work from home' kind of concept does not really exist in the career of a diplomat, which further intensified the gravity of the pandemic situation.

The birth of my daughter was a huge transition in my life. An immense blessing that one could crave for. We were entrenched with happiness. Finally, we were together, all four of us.

But soon, I started to realize that I was split into two halves. One half of me was riding on the joys of holding a new soul, a new being in my arms. The other half was diving into oceans of anxiety that came with the monotony of the situation.

My two contrasting selves made me analyse my life. It had become static due to months of lockdown and that had stopped my mental growth. I had decreased realization of my own potential.

It resulted in making me vulnerable to the stresses of life and I contributed less towards my family.

The COVID-19 crisis has hit human development hard, including fundamental elements such as income, education, health and, above all, social evolution.

Tough times challenge the most intricate part of any relationship. My supportive other half uplifts me and backs me to become the best version of me every day. He is my strongest motivation, my truest smile and my biggest comfort zone in all our ups and downs.

Two weeks after the birth of my daughter, my husband re-joined the office. I was alone to take care of a new-born and a toddler, but this time accompanied by postnatal blues.

Physically, I was in the healing process but mentally, I felt that every passing day was just adding further burden on my soul.

I grasped the reality that I cannot stop, no matter how bad I feel. I had to get out of my bed every day. I had to take care of my children. I had to do the household chores.

These months of psychological struggles have made me think that, even with the arrival of the vaccine, the pandemic is not going to end. A single dose of medicine circulating in our blood will not eradicate the psychological stresses that the human race has encountered. By the end of the pandemic, none of us will be the same. All of us will need self-renewal, internal healing and personal expansion. Travelling, meditation, work-life balance and self-reflection are going to be mandatory for mankind to heal. As we all repair and regenerate, that is how we learn, we grow, and we live.

After eight months of battling with emotions, blooming trees and vibrant flowers are indicating that another collision is impending. Yes, the winter is fading into spring. I am greeting this change with a much-altered perspective, somewhere more strong and somewhere more delicate and more vulnerable towards the anxiety.

It is a natural phenomenon that everything that happens to us, good or bad, teaches us lessons, and transform us into new beings. It helps us mould our lives ready for future challenges. Even this pandemic has taught us ways to live the new normal; to sit in our own company, enjoy our solitude and feel safe in our isolation. Society will change its dimensions after this pandemic. Friendships, relations, social circles, societal norms and practices are shifting to other paradigms. It gives us a chance to make our own selves better, to keep us away from negativities around us and to make this world safer and happier for generations to come.

I believe that the psychological pressures created by this virus will result in a forceful, composed and determined mental approach in our lives. It will help the human race design more beautiful ways to defeat stresses and pains in the future.

Now, I feel that an aura of hope is guarding my soul. Before her birth, it was the hope of meeting my daughter that kept me going. And now it is the hope that life is going to be regular and gentle again one day, the way It was before the pandemic. Along with these hopes and aspirations, there comes an end to our first posting and an end to one chapter of my life. But my heart will always long for this city as both of my children were born here and I have seen the most beautiful times and I have also seen the most resilient times here.

(Drazen Zigic/shutterstock.com)

16 The Male Diplomatic Spouses

These short stories are from the few interviews the editor conducted with male diplomatic spouses during her research project. It was perhaps not surprising that no male spouse could make it to this book given how gendered the spouses' world is even in contemporary diplomacy.

The Eternal Search for a Job

It took me a long time to get a job and when I got it, my quality of life dropped by seventy percent. As a family, we are settled. The only thing that following my wife's career has not done for me so far, is give me a job. The thing that I think is holding me back is the three-year career break I took in my wife's previous posting. So, I think I need to change my tactic on looking for work. I just need to take anything for two months and that will cover the gap. At the moment I have applied for 40 jobs and I had one rejection letter. That is the only contact that I have had. So, I think it is that three-year gap.

I tried and tried and tried to get a job. But after the first year, I sort of slowed down a bit. I worked out that if I were to go to work then we would need childcare. I took the childcare costs and grossed it up. I realized that the first 20,000 euros that I would earn would go straight out of the door. So, I reconsidered and stayed home.

I am trying to work out what to do. Something I could do without boredom and could do indefinitely. London might re-invigorate me. I might find a new job that I really enjoy.

Having a job and going there every day is incredibly important. I guess a lot of my happiness is based on achievements.

Who Follows Whom?

I was working in the UK first, before my wife got a posting here. I do not feel like a diplomatic spouse at all. Well, probably because I came here as an expat with my own job. I did not join her for her previous posting. So far, she has been following me and compromising her career to be with me. We have not done it in a 'normal' way yet. Whatever that is.

Half of me would be very happy to not work or to do charity work – the traditional spouse's things, you know. Teach language, teach English. Do all those sorts of things. I think that I never really had that experience and I do think that I would be bored, but we would miss my income as a family. It is not an option for me. Men are expected to work.

Go With the Flow
I kept telling everyone that, 'I am here for my wife, but nobody forced me, so I intend to make the most out of this opportunity and experience.' My wife was also responsible for North Korea when she was posted to China. So, I followed her to Pyongyang, helping her transfer all the things that she needed there. So, all of this was no problem at all. I could arrange time off from work with my company.

From China, my wife started looking at possibilities for the next posting, on the two continents that we had never visited, Africa and South America. In Africa, there was nothing interesting but in South America there was a post in Chile. I contacted some former colleagues of mine in the European company I used to work for. I asked about opportunities in South America in the company. There was Brazil, another country and then Chile. We were not interested in Brazil because we wanted Spanish speaking. And then this colleague of mine said, 'Chile is a really good one, you know.' My wife was really interested as well, so she applied to Chile. So, more or less, I landed from China to Chile with a job, going back to my old company.

I often think about being in this incredibly privileged situation, about our wives having diplomatic careers and us being able to follow them, explore and experience different things. When we were in China, there were a lot of people, surprisingly more women than men, who were feeling a bit sorry for me. They reassured me that I would find a job. But I did not worry about it. When we decided to go to China, I made the decision to go there for family, one hundred percent. I was not going against my will, so why worry once I was there?

Importance of Sports

The big thing for me with all the moving was that I lost my sports. The sports that I was used to were on TV at home, but not available anywhere else. It was difficult finding people who would like the same kind of sports as I do. Now they are on TV. It has been eleven years since I had rugby on my TV!

Countries we have lived in as a spouse

(www.spousesoftheworld.com/thebook)

About the Editor, Authors and Photographer

Editor

Dr Linn Eleanor Zhang is Lecturer at Loughborough University London researching expatriates, migrants and global workers from gender, language, and identity perspectives. She has published her research widely in academic journals such as *Gender, Work & Organization*, the *Journal of World Business* and *International Business Review*. Her book about expatriates' work lives, *Managing Expatriates in China: A Language and Identity Perspective*, is published by Palgrave Macmillan London. *Spouses of the World* is associated with her research project 'Gender and identity in a turbulent space and time' funded by British Academy/Leverhulme Small Research Grants.

Authors

Amy Richardson was born in Montréal, Canada. She studied Early Childhood Elementary Education, B.Ed. at Concordia University. Amy completed a post-graduate certificate in Teaching English as a Second Language (TESL) at McGill University and a Certificado in Espanol Avanzado at Université de Québec à Montréal. An elementary school teacher for fifteen years, she volunteers for a non-profit youth organization. Amy's blog *A Diplomat's Wife* tells the story of her posting in Honduras and teaching and parenting in Canada during the global pandemic. She is the mother of two young children and the wife of a Canadian diplomat working for Global Affairs Canada in international development.

Agnes Fenyvesy is a Hungarian senior civil servant working for the Centre of the National Tax and Customs Administration. She has been professionally published on taxation. She holds an MA in Public Administration, having graduated in Budapest, and attended the faculty of law. She is interested in the fields of human rights, and international and humanitarian law. She loves travelling, meeting people and experiencing different cultures. She enjoys being involved in international associations for diplomatic families, plays the piano and is a passionate amateur chef. She has lived in three different countries while accompanying her diplomat husband. Agnes speaks English, and has learnt Latin, Italian and German. She founded the Diplomatic Spouses Club in London (DSCL), and served as its President from 2014 until the end of 2017.

Britten Holter is the daughter of a diplomat and has lived in four countries – US, Sweden, UK and Estonia. Britten, born in Estonia, can identify herself as a multicultural child having experienced the varying ways of living in each of these countries. She can confidently say that this kind of a lifestyle has broadened her horizons and tested her ability to adapt. Britten has recently finished her bachelor's degree in Scotland and will continue her studies with a master's degree in Psychology.

Carmen Davies was born and brought up in Mexico City, where she studied accounting at university and married a British diplomat working there. She accompanied him during the rest of his posting in Mexico and later in Yugoslavia (Zagreb), Guatemala, Angola, Namibia and Panama. In between postings, she worked in London in the travel industry with American Airlines' Sabre Travel Information Network (STIN), Portuguese Airlines (TAP) and Lan-Chile. In London, she assisted the charity Children and Families Across Borders and helped to set up the Diplomatic Spouses Club in London (DSCL), for the spouses of foreign diplomats posted to London.

Emilia Atmanagara is an Indonesian-born Australian who emigrated to Australia with her parents at the age of two. Emilia is the mother of two children and grandmother of six, who has lived in Indonesia and the United Kingdom, accompanying her Australian diplomat spouse. Emilia has worked overseas and in Australia as a Senior Public Servant. While living abroad, she integrated into the local community by volunteering with local not-for-profit groups and mentoring young people. Now retired with her spouse Gerard, Emilia is enjoying family time and taking the opportunity to explore her home country.

Julia Gajewska-Pratt studied history, anthropology and education at Adelaide University, and has post-graduate qualifications in multicultural education and linguistics. She has taught in Australia, Malaysia, Indonesia and Cambodia. She represented Australia at the Asia-Pacific Ladies Friendship Society in Japan and was also Vice President of the Japanese branch of the Australian & New Zealand Association (ANZA). A trained Guide at the National Gallery of Australia (NGA), she also trained Guides at the Museum National Jakarta. She was actively involved with the Indonesian Heritage Society running a study group, organising tours and fundraising for Indonesian cultural institutions. On returning to Australia in 2010 from Indonesia, she committed to independent Asian art research based upon her interest in collecting and researching textiles from South East Asia, Japan and South Asia and working and Guiding at the NGA. She also undertook postgraduate study in Asian art at SOAS University of London in 2015-17. She has also researched and published on Sri Lankan batik whilst living in Colombo in 2018/19. She currently resides in Delhi with her husband on their eighth overseas posting.

Manca Rupel is the daughter of a diplomatic couple and has escorted her family to three different countries since childhood. She finished kindergarten in the US, spent most of her primary school years in Slovenia and finished her secondary education in the United Kingdom. Currently, she studies Human Biology at Loughborough University in the UK.

Marzia Brofferio Celeste made her first move when she was four-years-old and has not stopped since. She attended the European School in Bergen (Netherlands) and graduated in Business Administration at L. Bocconi University in Milan. She worked at the EU in Brussels and as a Head-hunter and Management Consultant with international companies. Married to an Italian diplomat since 1994 and the mother of two children, she is a passionate reader and collaborates at *Altrov'è*, the official magazine of the Italian Ministry of Foreign Affairs' Spouses Association. She sings in the Italian Ministry of Foreign Affairs' Women's Choir and with them she has recorded a CD of international Christmas songs. She is active in the parents' association in her children's schools and speaks four languages. She has lived in Italy, the Netherlands, France, Belgium, Syria, Bulgaria and the UK.

M Mohammed is an architectural engineer. Her work is based on designing small houses and buildings, refurbishing and extending old houses and project managing. A mother of two, she does voluntary cooking for fifty-plus people at religious events. As the spouse of a diplomat, she has lived in three different countries and has planned many cultural and social events.

She has visited almost thirty different cities around the world in twelve years. M speaks Arabic, English and a little Farsi. She likes drawing and teaching herself new languages.

Dr Monica Pavese Rubins graduated in Humanities and further specialised in Classical Archaeology at University of Turin. She received a PhD in Ancient History from University of Nice-Sophia Antipolis in 2006. She has been a Fellow of the Royal Historical Society since 2017. She is the author of several articles and two books. Born in Sweden of Italian-born parents, she grew up in Italy. She studied in six European countries. She worked at the Embassy of Italy in Stockholm on the promotion of Italian Science and Research abroad. She has been a diplomatic spouse at the Embassy of Latvia in two countries and she is the mother of a lovely trilingual child. She was President of the Diplomatic Spouses Club in London (DSCL) in 2019. At present, she is a tenured teacher of the Italian Language, Literature and History in Italy, but her travelling bags are always ready.

Nina Rousu is a casual adventurer, a mother of two and an author from Finland. Her husband works for the British Foreign, Commonwealth and Development Office. Nina has lived in thirteen countries and, with her husband, she has been posted to Canada, Uganda, Kenya, Finland, UK and, at the time of writing, India.

Dr Ilona Kenkadze holds a PhD in the field of linguistics of the English language. She enjoys teaching English grammar to Georgian and international students, and working as an Associate Professor at two Universities in Tbilisi: Georgian National University and Tbilisi State University. Her works on teaching English have been published in international journals. Being married to a Georgian diplomat, Ilona accompanied her husband and travelled with their two sons during his service, actively playing an essential part in all aspects of family adaptation and, at the same time, maintaining and enhancing her professional knowledge and teaching skills by regularly participating in scientific linguistic and language learning conferences. She speaks perfect Georgian, English and Russian, loves swimming and her current hobbies are drawing and winemaking.

Olga Lucia Lozano has been an international trade expert for over 29 years. She contributed to the institutional development in her country, Colombia, in the defence of export interests in different markets, and the strengthening of the Colombian role in the international arena. She has also lived in Chile, Switzerland and the United Kingdom due to her job as a Minister Counsellor of the WTO Colombian Mission and as the wife of a Chilean diplomat. Currently, she resides in Bogotá, Colombia where she works as a private consultant and sits on management boards. She is the proud mother of a 23-year-old son. She has combined her professional career with experiences in London as a care worker and a volunteer in Westminster Cathedral and the Paddington Homework Club. Recently, she became a logotherapy coach.

Dr Ratna Roshida Ab Razak is Associate Professor at the Department of Government and Civilizational Studies at the Universiti Putra Malaysia. She earned her BA in Human Sciences (Hons) in 1995 from the International Islamic University Malaysia, her MA (1996) and her PhD (2000) from Leeds University, UK. Her areas of interest are civilizational studies and humanistic psychology, which she formalized in her PhD and resulted in her book *Understanding Al-Mutanabbi: A Humanistic Psychological Approach.* Her main research area is about spirituality, meaning, purpose and values in life and civilizational studies. She has presented papers at conferences internationally, published articles and papers and contributed a chapter to the book *Civilizational Competencies and Regional Development in Poland* (Warsaw University Press, 2009). She has been on unpaid leave for three years, accompanying her husband at the Malaysian High Commission in London.

Dr Valentina Prevolnik Rupel is Senior Researcher at the Institute for Economic Research in Ljubljana, Slovenia. She is also Associate Professor at the DOBA Faculty in Maribor, the first Slovenian fully online faculty. She was part of the Minister of Health's cabinet and was an advisor to the Health Insurance Institute of Slovenia's CEO. Her research focuses on health care financing models, health technology assessment, health-related quality of life health outcomes as well as long-term care financing. She has published extensively in international academic journals. She is involved in many international and national research projects. Originally from Slovenia, her role as a diplomatic spouse provided her an opportunity to live in three countries for extended time periods.

Dr Zoofa Talha is a dentist, the wife of a Pakistani diplomat and the mother of two children. She graduated from the Army Medical College (National University of Science and Technology), Pakistan. Later, she trained in dentistry as a military house officer. She has also taught medical students in Riphah International University, Pakistan. As an active community dentist, she has spent time in clinic as well as travelling around the state to encourage healthy habits in young students. Additionally, she has been involved in dentistry research programmes and has an international research publication. She made her first diplomatic move to Argentina where she travelled, explored and analysed the culture. Her horizon has diversified from the boundaries of dentistry to evaluating new culture and languages. She has learnt Spanish and also Teaching English as a Foreign Language (TEFL).

Photographer
Margarita Mavromichalis is a photographer who comes from a family of Greek diplomats and has spent her life living and travelling all over the world. She speaks five languages and studied translation and interpreting.
Margarita moved to New York in 2009. She continued her studies at the International Center of Photography. In Greece from 2013 to 2016, she devoted most of her work to covering the refugee crisis as it developed on the island of Lesvos. Margarita is attracted to street photography and the elements that evoke emotions and surprise in our everyday life. She is passionate about documenting current events, highlighting their social impact. Her work has been displayed in exhibitions in New York, Boston, The Museum of the City of New York, the Brooklyn Historical Society and, most recently, in Budapest, Athens, Paris, Berlin, Barcelona and London. Selected images are part of the permanent collections of the Museum of the City of New York and the Brooklyn Historical Society. She won the 9th Pollux Awards (2016) and the 12th edition of the Julia Margaret Cameron Awards (2018); was a finalist at the Miami Street Photography Festival (2018); was nominated for the 2019 Prix Pictet Hope Award and was awarded the 15th edition of the Julia Margaret Cameron Award (2020).

Sabrestorm Stories is a hybrid publisher dedicated to producing beautiful books for authors who choose to work with industry professionals to bring their words to the public. We offer bespoke publishing options for discerning authors with dreams of seeing their book in print, whether for their family or for a wider audience, in the genres of biography and memoir, self-help, general non-fiction and fiction.

SABRESTORM
STORIES

Website: www.sabrestormstories.com
Email: enquiries@sabrestormstories.co.uk